AF334076

*Classics in
Maritime History*

William N. Still, Jr., *Editor*

What Finer Tradition

Thomas O. Selfridge, Jr., about 1886.

WHAT FINER TRADITION:

The Memoirs of Thomas O. Selfridge, Jr., Rear Admiral, U.S.N.

with a new introduction by
William N. Still, Jr.

University of South Carolina Press

Copyright © University of South Carolina 1987

Published in Columbia, South Carolina, by the
University of South Carolina Press

Manufactured in the United States of America

Library of Congess Cataloging-in-Publication Data

Selfridge, T. O. (Thomas Oliver), 1836–1924.
  What finer tradition.

  Reprint. Originally published: New York:
Knickerbocker Press, 1924, under title: Memoirs
of Thomas O. Selfridge, Jr., Rear Admiral, U.S.N.
  Bibliography: p.
  1. Selfridge, T. O. (Thomas Oliver), 1836–1924.
2. United States—History, Naval. 3. United States.
Navy—History. 4. United States—History—Civil
War, 1861–1865—Naval operations. 5. Admirals—
United States—Biography. 6. United States.
Navy—Biography. I. Title.
E182.S47 1987 359.3'331'0924 [B] 86-30706
ISBN 0-87249-507-8

Contents

INTRODUCTION

Rear Admiral Thomas O. Selfridge, Jr., is not a well-known naval officer. Yet during the Civil War he commanded the *Monitor* and the experimental submarine *Alligator*, and had the unwanted distinction of being the only Union naval officer during the war to have three ships sunk under him. The *Cumberland* went down while engaging the Confederate iron-clad *Virginia* during the March 8, 1862, battle in Hampton Roads; the monitor *Cairo* sank in the Yazoo River after a torpedo exploded under her hull; and the gunboat *Conestoga* was lost in the Mississippi River after a collision. Although Selfridge would retire from the Navy just before the beginning of the Spanish-American War, the Civil War was *the* war. In fact Selfridge would never again engage in combat after 1865.

Thomas O. Selfridge, Jr., was the son of a distinguished naval officer, Captain Thomas Oliver Selfridge, Sr. The father entered the Navy in 1818 and commanded a number of ships and naval stations before retiring in 1866. He died in 1903 at the age of ninety-eight, one of the oldest officers ever carried on the Navy List. The British Admiralty ordered their ships and stations to fly their flags at half mast in his memory, the oldest admiral in the world when he died.

The son was born on February 6, 1836, in Charlestown, Massachusetts. Selfridge would later write in his *Memoirs* that virtually from the cradle it was assumed that he would follow his father in a naval career. His formal training commenced when he entered the Naval Academy at Annapolis in 1851. Selfridge was the first officer to receive a diploma under the permanent Naval Academy system when he graduated in 1854 at the head of his class of six. Because of the need for more junior officers, his class graduated a year early.

Soon after graduation, Midshipman Selfridge reported on board the *Independence* in New York City, preparing for a cruise as flagship to the Pacific Squadron. During the following two years, the *Independence* sailed around the Horn, to California, and from there to the Hawaiian Islands, Samoa, Chile, and Panama. Josiah Tattnall, who would later command the Confederate ironclad *Virginia*, was the *Independence*'s captain. Selfridge referred to Tattnall as a gunnery "sharp" and gave him credit for developing his expertise in gunnery. Selfridge, throughout his career, would place a considerable emphasis on gunnery practice.

The young midshipman apparently impressed his commanding officer, for he was assigned as a regular watch and division officer, the only midshipman other than "passed midshipmen" so assigned.

In the fall of 1856, he was ordered to Washington, D.C., where he successfully passed his examination for promotion to passed midshipman. Two years later, he would be advanced to the rank of master.

In January, 1857, Selfridge was ordered to the Coast Survey schooner *Nautilus*. There were not enough billets available for the entire officer corps in the late 1850s; therefore, a large number of officers were assigned to coast survey work, engaged in charting the rivers and harbors throughout the United States. The *Nautilus*, with Selfridge as acting master, surveyed the Rappahannock River in Virginia and the Hudson in New York before he received orders as master to the sloop *Vincennes* in the African Squadron. Survey work was considered tedious and boring work by most naval officers, but it did provide them with much-needed experience in handling small vessels.

The African Squadron had been established in the 1840s to aid in the suppression of the foreign slave trade. Because of the prevalence of yellow fever and malaria and the lack of attractive liberty ports, the African Squadron was universally disliked throughout the service. It was considered the least desirable of all the foreign stations. For two and a half years, Selfridge served on the *Vincennes*:

This cruise was a very unpleasant one, on account not only of the climate and the isolation, but also the unsociability, not to say tyranny, of our Captain. All of the ship's officers were constantly harassed by him and often placed under suspension. My principal duty was that of navigator, though frequently it was necessary to take a watch when the other officers were sick.

Selfridge concluded his account by saying that "this cruise was the most unpleasant one of my experience."

In the summer of 1860 Selfridge was promoted to lieutenant and shortly afterwards was ordered to the frigate *Cumberland*, flagship of the Home Squadron. The Home Squadron included all commissioned vessels stationed on the Atlantic and Gulf coasts.

Selfridge was on the *Cumberland* when the Civil War began. In April, the frigate was at the Gosport Navy Yard at Norfolk for repairs. When the yard was abandoned, Selfridge was detailed with a small number of men from the *Cumberland* to destroy equipment and facilities to keep them out of Confederate hands. As the yard was set on fire the *Cumberland*, in tow of a small steamer, was taken down the mouth of the Elizabeth River and out into Hampton Roads.

The *Cumberland* was employed in blockading the entrance to the James and Elizabeth rivers throughout the late spring and early summer of 1861. After a brief refit at the Boston Navy Yard, she was ordered to join the naval force off Hatteras Inlet, North Carolina. In August the *Cumberland*, along with other Union naval vessels, bombarded the two forts guarding the inlet. When the forts surrendered, the frigate returned to Hampton Roads and anchored in the mouth of the James River. There she was joined by the *Congress* to blockade the river. Six months later the two vessels were still on station near the river's mouth when the Confederate iron-clad *Virginia* made her appearance.

At 12:45 P.M. on March 8, 1862, lookouts on both the *Cumberland* and *Congress* observed three Confederate vessels steaming out of the Elizabeth River. As they got nearer, it was discovered that one of the vessels was the *Virginia*, converted by the rebels from the wooden sloop-of-war *Mer-*

rimack. Both ships promptly beat to quarters and cleared for action.

The Union vessels had ample time to prepare for battle, because the slow-moving iron-clad took slightly more than an hour to steam within firing range. The *Virginia*'s commanding officer intended to ram the *Cumberland* first—she had a much heavier battery than the *Congress*—then turn on the *Congress*. The *Cumberland* was anchored 800 yards from the shore, lying athwart the river with her bow outward, an unfortunate position because she could not be swung to meet her opponent. The *Cumberland* opened fire as soon as her guns could be brought to bear; the *Virginia* replied and as the iron-clad closed, the two vessels continued to exchange fire. The *Cumberland* definitely received the worst of it. Shots bounced off the iron-clad's armor while shells from the *Virginia* penetrated the Union vessel's fragile hull and exploded among her crew. One shot alone wiped out a sixteen-man crew. After raking the helpless wooden vessel for a few minutes, the *Virginia* rammed the *Cumberland*'s starboard side, crushing her hull directly below the berth deck. Upon impact the iron-clad fired one of her bow rifles into the stricken ship, killing ten men. The *Cumberland* began immediately to settle by the bow with a list to port. She nearly dragged the *Virginia* down, too, for the ram had stuck in the victim's hull. However, the ram broke and the ironclad was able to back clear.

During the engagement Selfridge was in charge of the frigate's forward battery of six guns. He wrote in his *Memoirs* that even after the *Virginia* had rammed the Union warship and she was obviously sinking, the *Cumberland*'s acting commanding officer, Lieutenant George N. Morris, refused to surrender. For nearly half an hour, until it was impossible to elevate the guns, he continued to fight. Selfridge's description of the battle and the *Cumberland*'s loss is described in his *Memoirs*.

After Selfridge and the other survivors had reached the beach, according to one account, he saw the *Cumberland*'s flag still flying at the masthead and with a small group of volunteers returned to the sinking ship and retrieved the flag. Another account by one of the *Cumberland*'s officers mentioned that, while the survivors were standing on the beach,

the *Merrimack* again opened fire on the Congress. The shells were flying over our heads in a very uncomfortable manner, when we met Lieutenant Selfridge near some large trees. A shell came whizzing along, passing over our heads and the pilot and I involuntarily ducked our heads and each of us got behind a good-sized tree, seeing which Lieutenant Selfridge, who was very much affected, said "Don't dodge, I wish one would kill me; I'd rather be killed than be whipped. . . ."

Selfridge did not mention either incident in his *Memoirs*. He did write,

Furious over the loss of the ship in which I had taken such intense pride, shivering with cold from soaking wet and scanty clothing, the reaction from the long endured, frightful, experiences of battle impelled me to tears, and I sobbed like a child.

That evening Selfridge remained on the beach and the following day he, along with thousands of others lining both sides of Hampton Roads, witnessed the *Monitor–Virginia* engagement. After the battle was over, the *Cumberland* and *Congress* survivors were taken out to the *Roanoke*, the flagship of Captain John Marston, the senior officer present. Leave was granted to the survivors, including Selfridge. Before he was able to depart, however,

a message came from Mr. Fox, the Assistant Secretary of the Navy, who had come down from Washington on receipt of news of the *Merrimac* episode, that he wished to see me. Captain Marston had recommended me for the command of the *Monitor* in place of Lieutenant Worden, who had been wounded in the fight, and the Secretary offered me the honor. . . . I thanked him for his confidence and replied that, "if the *Merrimac* comes out, the *Monitor* will be on hand."

That evening after reporting on board, Selfridge, accompanied by Engineer Alban L. Stimers, spent more than four hours thoroughly examining the *Monitor* from stem to stern. Selfridge would only command the *Monitor* for four days and says very little about this period in his *Memoirs*. He did write that

Early next morning [the day after assuming command], we proceeded to a position off the mouth of the Elizabeth River, and remained without being rewarded by a sight of the *Merrimac*.

On March 13 Lieutenant William N. Jeffers was ordered to relieve Selfridge in command of the *Monitor*. Selfridge then went on a month's leave and upon returning to Hampton Roads was given command of the *Illinois*, a large coastal steamer chartered by the government. Again the command only lasted a few days, as the vessel's charter was revoked. He then became flag lieutenant on the staff of Flag Officer Louis M. Goldsborough, in command of the North Atlantic Blockading Squadron. In this position he carried out a number of tasks including taking orders to various ship commanders and, after the occupation of Norfolk, the destruction of abandoned Confederate batteries in the vicinity of the port.

In July Goldsborough resigned as flag officer, and Selfridge went to Washington hoping to obtain orders to command a ship. Once again it was Assistant Secretary of the Navy Fox who responded to the young officer's plea. Fox offered him command of the most unorthodox vessel in the Navy at that time, the *Alligator*. The *Alligator*, which "resembled a whale in external form," was a submarine. The vessel was built in Philadelphia during the fall and winter of 1861–62. She was 45 feet in length and $4\frac{1}{2}$ feet in the beam, built along the lines of a steamship boiler with a riveted hull. Her propulsion consisted of eight oars on each side. On June 13, 1862, the Navy accepted the submarine from her builder. Shortly afterwards, she was towed to Hampton Roads, but no suitable "target" could be found. Goldsborough considered the *Alligator* useless and obtained permission to send her to the Washington Navy Yard for further testing. The submarine was still at the yard when Selfridge received orders to command her.

Selfridge commanded the *Alligator* less than two weeks. He carried out a series of tests and on August 8 reported to the Department that "the enterprise is a failure." He had difficulty in controlling the vessel while submerged and stressed that she was extremely slow on the surface, unable to stem the tide. Selfridge and his entire crew, all volunteers, requested transfer and on August 9, he was ordered to take his men to Cairo, Illinois. (The *Alligator* was later lost off Hatteras while being towed to Charleston.) At Cairo, Selfridge received the good news that he had been promoted to lieutenant commander and also that he was ordered to command the monitor *Cairo*.

Selfridge took command of the *Cairo* at Memphis, Tennessee. She was 175 feet long, $51\frac{1}{2}$ feet in the beam with a 6-foot draft. Her battery of thirteen guns was inclosed in an iron armored casemate. The *Cairo* was one of seven gunboats of the type called the "City Class" because they were named after western river ports.

During the first three months of Selfridge's command, the *Cairo* patrolled the Mississippi River, occasionally exchanging rifle and cannon fire with Confederate guerillas. On November 21, Rear Admiral David Porter, in command of the Mississippi Squadron, detailed the *Cairo* to an expedition being formed to attack Vicksburg, Mississippi. As a preliminary to this expedition, the *Cairo* was ordered to ascend the Yazoo River, which flowed into the Mississippi ten miles above Vicksburg, and clear the stream of mines. On December 12, 1862, Selfridge in the *Cairo* led a small flotilla of gunboats up the winding Yazoo. At approximately mid-morning the *Cairo* struck two mines. Her bow was lifted out of the water by the explosion. As the vessel began to settle, Selfridge shoved her into the bank. In twelve minutes the *Cairo* was completely submerged except for her stacks.

Although no lives were lost and only a few men were slightly wounded, the loss of the *Cairo* earned Selfridge considerable criticism. A fellow officer wrote, "On December 12 Lieutenant Commander Selfridge . . . found two torpedoes and removed them by placing his vessel over them." Admiral Porter informed the Navy Department of the vessel's loss and remarked that the *Cairo* "incautiously proceeded too far ahead . . . when the torpedo exploded under her." He accused Selfridge of disobeying orders and added, "My own opinion is that due caution was not observed." The admiral, however, apparently impressed with Selfridge's aggressiveness, later withdrew his censure: "I can see in it nothing more than one of the accidents of war arising from a zealous disposition on the part of the commanding officer to perform his duty." When Selfridge reported to Porter on his flagship, he asked the admiral if a court of inquiry was to be held. Porter replied, "Court! I have no time to order courts. I can't blame an officer who puts his ship close to the enemy. Is there any other vessel you would like to have?" Selfridge was then ordered to assume command of the *Conestoga*, whose commanding officer had recently been detached because of ill health.

Porter informed the Navy Department, "I have put . . . [Selfridge] in command of the *Conestoga* . . . , trusting that he may be more fortunate hereafter, this being the second time during the war that his vessel had gone down under him."

Selfridge commanded the side-wheeler for five months. During most of this period she patrolled the Mississippi River in the vicinity of the Arkansas and White rivers. Porter had divided up the Mississippi River and its tributaries into areas of responsibility and assigned units of his squadron to designated areas. The vessels were to patrol their assigned areas and protect shipping. According to Selfridge, his most notable achievement while in command of the *Conestoga* was to change the course of the Mississippi River. At the mouth of the Arkansas River was a long, narrow point projecting into the

Mississippi, making an eighteen-mile turn necessary to get around it. This had become a favorite spot for guerillas to attack transports. One morning Selfridge noticed that much of the neck was flooded because of unusually high water and came to the conclusion that the channel might be diverted by digging a small ditch linking the flooded water. He put his crew to work with shovels and a small ditch was dug. It worked. By the following morning, the Mississippi was rapidly cutting through the neck, and within a few weeks it was wide and deep enough for vessels to follow that channel.

On the whole, however, Selfridge found his duty "monotonous, and ... rather irksome, particularly since I felt that the unfortunate loss of the *Cairo* had kept me from participating in [the expedition against Vicksburg]." In May, 1863, the *Conestoga* needed to go north for repairs. Selfridge and his crew were transferred to the side-wheel gunboat *Manitou*. Less than two weeks after taking over the *Manitou*, he heard that General William T. Sherman had requested a battery of naval guns. The guns were to be landed and installed in positions to be used against the Confederates defending Vicksburg. Selfridge, anxious for more active service, immediately volunteered to command the guns. Porter approved and the *Mani-*

tou's two 8-inch guns were landed early in June. From then until the end of the siege and surrender of Vicksburg, the battery fired constantly on Confederate positions. More than a thousand rounds were fired and at least two Confederate cannon were put out of action. On the first of July, four days before the town's surrender, Selfridge was ordered to return to the *Conestoga*, which had rejoined the naval force near Vicksburg.

Shortly after resuming command of the *Conestoga*, Selfridge was ordered by Porter to lead a raid up the Red River. In addition to the *Conestoga*, the force consisted of the gunboats *Manitou*, *Rattler*, *Forest Rose*, *Petrel*, and *Curlew*. For the first time, Selfridge was appointed to command an expedition. The object was to capture cotton and supplies as well as to disperse any Confederate forces along the river. The expedition was most successful. Entering the Red River the gunboats turned into the Black River and afterwards into the Tensas River. Selfridge's small flotilla also reached Lake Tensas and the Little Red River, another tributary of the Red. Four steamers were destroyed, together with a large quantity of ammunition and provisions.

After this expedition, the *Conestoga* · returned to patrolling the Mississippi River.

On March 8, 1864, she collided with the steamer *General Price* and sank in about four minutes. "Thus for the third time in the war, I had had my ship suddenly sunk under me," Selfridge wrote in his *Memoirs*. He added, "It is a strange coincidence that the names of these three ships all begin with the letter 'C'." Admiral Porter, in some disgust, said, "Well, Selfridge, you do not seem to have much luck with the top of the alphabet." Selfridge was then placed in command of the iron-clad *Osage*, far from the "top of the alphabet."

He assumed command of the *Osage* two days after losing the *Conestoga*. The *Osage* was a river monitor, but unlike other monitors, she and her two sister ships were propelled by stern wheels. Unfortunately, their wheels, protected by armored casings, made it impossible for the turrets to turn a full 360 degrees. The *Osage* was an unusual-looking vessel with virtually nothing showing above the waterline but the turret, the iron-plated house for the stern paddle wheel, and the tall thin stacks.

Shortly after Selfridge took her over, the *Osage* joined other warships in Admiral Porter's squadron on the Red River expedition. On January 4, 1864, Major General Henry W. Hallack wrote Major General Nathaniel P. Banks, "General Sherman and Steel agree with me in opinion that the Red River is the shortest and best ... base of operations against Texas." Banks was ordered to "operate in that direction," as soon as there was "sufficient water." Late in March, Bank's army of approximately 36,000 men started towards Shreveport, their line of march paralleling the Red River and Porter's squadron of thirteen gunboats. Passage up the narrow and crooked river was difficult and dangerous; the water was low and at places obstructed. Near Alexandria, approximately halfway to Shreveport, there were rapids, choked with rocks that seriously impeded navigation. Taking advantage of a rise in the river, Porter's vessels, including the *Osage*, passed through the rapids, but could go little farther. On April 8–9, 1864, Banks' army was defeated and turned back in two battles. His troops began to retire downstream and Porter had no choice but to do the same with his vessels.

The admiral left Selfridge in charge of a rearguard division of four light iron-clads several miles above Alexandria while the rest of the squadron passed through the rapids above Alexandria. Because the river was so low a dam had to be built to enable the gunboats to pass through the rapids. Selfridge's vessels were to prevent any Confederate effort to attack the squadron while this was going on. All but one of Porter's large gunboats made it through the rapids safely, followed shortly afterwards by the four light iron-clads.

With the end of the unfortunate Red River expedition, the *Osage* returned to patrolling the Mississippi. However, in May Selfridge was given command of a new vessel, the recently completed ram *Vindicator*. He also remained in command of a division of gunboats which had the responsibility for patrolling a small segment of the river. By the late summer of 1864, nearly all Confederate resistance, including guerilla attacks, had ceased. Selfridge, bored with the lack of activity, requested a transfer. Admiral Porter had recently been ordered to command the North Atlantic Blockading Squadron and intervened to get Selfridge sent to his squadron.

In October Selfridge was ordered to command the gunboat *Huron*, a small vessel of 700 tons with a battery of one 11-inch gun and a 30-pounder Parrott. Shortly after he assumed the command, the *Huron* was ordered to join the blockade off the Cape Fear River in North Carolina. The Cape Fear connects the port of Wilmington with the Atlantic Ocean. By 1864 Wilmington had become the most important center of blockade running in the Southern states. Two forts, Caswell and Fisher, guarded the river mouth. Fort Fisher was considered by many to be the most powerful fort in the Confederacy. The Navy had more than once urged that the forts be seized by amphibious assault, but until the fall of 1864 the Army was unable or unwilling to provide troops. In the fall, however, priority was given to attacking Fort Fisher. The Army made troops available and Admiral Porter assembled a powerful fleet to provide support.

On Christmas Eve, 1864, Porter's fleet bombarded the fort, firing more than 20,000 shells. The *Huron* participated in the attack. The bombardment, however, proved fruitless. The Army commander, Major General Benjamin Butler, refused to land his troops. Porter, chagrined at this failure, immediately made plans to launch a second attack. On January 12, 1865, his fleet once again opened fire on the fort. During the following days more than 8,000 troops under Major General Alfred H. Terry landed under the fire of Porter's guns. On January 15, a Sunday, 2,000 sailors and marines landed and attacked the seaward face of the fort while Terry's men assaulted from the land. Selfridge, in the thick of things as usual, commanded one of the units of bluejackets and marines in the landing party.

Fort Fisher fell, although as Selfridge

points out in his *Memoirs*, the landing party of marines and sailors was repulsed. A few days later Caswell also fell, opening the river to Porter's ships. Selfridge, back on the *Huron* after the survivors of the landing party had returned to ship, was ordered to anchor in the mouth of the Cape Fear River. The *Huron* was fortunate enough to capture two blockade runners that had entered the river, not suspecting that the forts had fallen. After Wilmington was occupied by Federal troops, the *Huron* was ordered to the James River to cooperate with Union forces moving on Richmond. The gunboat participated in no action, however, and she was still in the river when Richmond surrendered early in April, 1865. The news of Jefferson Davis' flight led Porter to order Selfridge to Key West, Florida, with the *Huron* to intercept the Confederate president if he tried to flee the country in that direction. After this, the *Huron* returned to New York City and was placed out of commission.

Selfridge had spent virtually the entire Civil War period on active service, most of it in combat zones. He had participated in numerous engagements, had had three ships sunk under him, and had been mentioned frequently in reports to the Department. As a naval officer who served with him wrote, Selfridge "has lived a good while for a young man." He was twenty-nine years old when the war ended.

Upon being detached from the *Huron*, Selfridge was ordered to report as executive officer to the *Hartford*, at that time preparing to leave for the Asiatic station. He requested shore duty in order to get married and was assigned to the Naval Academy as an instructor in the Department of Seamanship. In the fall of 1865 he married Ellen F. Shepley. They were to have four sons. She died in 1905, and two years later he married Gertrude Wildes. While at the academy Selfridge was placed in command of the old *Macedonian*, which had been relegated to a training ship for midshipmen during the summer months. Practice cruises were made along the Atlantic coast and to Europe. A junior officer on the *Macedonian* wrote that Selfridge "was an excellent officer, and while under his command the old *Macedonian* was a model in making passage from port to port."

After three years of what Selfridge described as "very pleasant duty" at the Naval Academy, he was ordered to command the steam gunboat *Nipsic*. Selfridge's tour on the *Nipsic* lasted nearly two years, most of which was spent in the West Indies. At that time the United States was considered the establishment of a naval base in the Caribbean and Selfridge investigated possible sites in Cuba, Santo Domingo, and Haiti.

In December, 1869, he was promoted to commander and ordered to conduct a survey of the Isthmus of Darien for an interoceanic canal. Selfridge would lead three expeditions to the Darien region between 1870 and 1873. Enduring unfriendly inhabitants, tropical fevers, rampaging rivers, and at times impenetrable vegetation, Selfridge's small command explored all the country south of Panama to the headwaters of the Alrato River in South America. The expeditions also surveyed a route that was considered feasible for a canal to link the Atlantic with the Pacific. For several years Selfridge would push for the adoption of his proposed route but with no success. For his work on the Darien survey, Selfridge was awarded the decoration of the Legion of Honor of France and made an honorary member of the Royal Geographical Society of Belgium. He was also invited by Ferdinand de Lesseps to attend a congress of interoceanic canals in Paris.

After a three-year tour at the Boston Navy Yard, Selfridge was given command of the *Enterprise* in 1878 and ordered to survey the Amazon and Madeira rivers. The object was to prove the navigability of the great South American river system and open to American commerce the interior of Brazil. After completing this mission, the *Enterprise* was ordered to join the European Squadron for a two-year tour.

In November, 1880, he was promoted to captain and ordered to take charge of the Naval Torpedo Station at Newport, Rhode Island. In the 1860s, Robert Whitehead, an Englishman, had developed an automotive torpedo. Whitehead torpedoes were used extensively during the Russo-Turkish War of 1877–1878 by the Russian Navy, which used small fast "torpedo boats" to launch attacks against larger vessels. The Russian success persuaded the U.S. Navy to experiment with Whitehead torpedoes, and the station at Newport was established for this purpose. During the four years that Selfridge commanded the station, numerous experiments with torpedoes, torpedo nets, and torpedo-carrying craft were conducted. Selfridge considered that his experiments led to the Navy's adopting these weapons.

In 1885 he was given command of the screw-sloop *Omaha*, which left in the spring of that year for an extended tour of duty with the Asiatic Squadron. An incident occurred during this cruise that resulted in Selfridge being court-martialed. While in Japanese waters he held target practice, and a Japanese man was injured when he picked up an unexploded shell fired at a cliff by the *Omaha*. An unusual sequence of events followed. Selfridge's report on the incident resulted in his detachment from command of the *Omaha* and being ordered to Washington, D.C. The Secretary of the Navy ordered him back to Japan, where an inquiry would be held; and finally Selfridge himself demanded a court-martial. He was acquitted by the court.

In 1889 Selfridge was ordered to Washington as a member of the Board of Inspection and Survey. The board at that time was involved in conducting trials on some of the first steel ships in the Navy. He was then ordered to head a commission to select a site for a navy yard in Puget Sound on the West Coast. Brementon was recommended and approved. In 1890 Selfridge was appointed commandant of the Boston Navy Yard and was still in command of the yard in 1894 when he was promoted to commodore.

In 1895 Selfridge was ordered to command the European Squadron. He received this prestigious command because no rear admirals were available and he was in line for promotion to that rank. He was commissioned a rear admiral the following year.

The European Squadron was the successor to the Mediterranean Squadron and had been established during the Civil War. It was the most popular of the distant squadrons because of the attractive liberty ports. Selfridge himself would refer to this tour with the squadron as "almost like yachting."

When Selfridge assumed command, the squadron consisted of two armored cruisers, the *Marblehead* and the *San Francisco*. Shortly after taking over the squadron in November, he was ordered to the Ottoman Empire "to personally investigate and report fully on the danger to American missionaries." The danger referred to concerned Turkish atrocities against Armenians. American missionaries had established schools, hospitals, and churches in a number of Armenian villages and had reported to diplomatic and church officials that they were in some danger. The Armenian massacres in Anatolia and other parts of the Ottoman Empire had caused a storm of protest in Europe and the United States. It was fear for the lives of the missionaries in Turkey that prompted the United States government to order warships to the eastern Mediterranean. Even before Selfridge arrived to command the squadron, the *Marblehead* was patrolling off the Ottoman coast.

Shortly after he arrived in the Near East, Selfridge reported that the missionaries were, in his opinion, in no immediate danger. Nevertheless, apparently under pressure from missionary interests in the United States, a third armored cruiser, the *Minneapolis*, was ordered to join the European Squadron in the eastern Mediterranean. Early in June, 1895, Selfridge received instructions to concentrate his squadron at Alexandretta, Syria, to evacuate all Americans and to "land a force," if necessary. The Americans, mostly missionaries, refused to take refuge on the warships and Selfridge continued to insist that they were in no immediate danger.

In the spring of 1896, Selfridge departed with two of his vessels, planning to attend the coronation of Tsar Nicholas II. The *Marblehead* was left in the eastern Mediterranean to evacuate Americans if necessary. In May the squadron sailed for Cronstadt. There the admiral and many of his officers journeyed to Moscow, where they participated in the pomp and pageantry surrounding the coronation of the last Romanov ruler of Imperial Russia. The squadron remained a month in Russian waters and then visited Denmark and England before returning to the eastern Mediterranean in August. Selfridge never changed his opinion concerning the lack of danger for the missionaries. He was also critical of the policy of deploying the European Squadron in Turkish waters for extended periods. Nevertheless, he was instructed to keep at least one of his vessels in the eastern Mediterranean at all times.

Admiral Selfridge's tour in command of the European Squadron was scheduled to end in August, 1897, but the department agreed to allow him to remain until he reached the statutory age of retirement, sixty-two. On February 6, 1898, only a couple of months before war broke out with Spain, Selfridge hauled down his flag from the *San Francisco* and relinquished command of the squadron. This ended a career of forty-seven years in the Navy.

Selfridge was considered an excellent squadron commander by his officers, but his "by the book" or no-nonsense attitude was at times considered to be excessive by subordinates. As a squadron commander, he personally examined the ships' logs, and when a discrepancy was found, the commanding officer would be reprimanded. Even spelling was corrected. He constantly wrote his commanders expressing disapproval of any actions that deviated even slightly from regulations. He personally conducted weekly inspections of the vessels under his command, writing long, detailed reports of their conditions. Should one man fail inspection, he would cancel liberty for the entire ship's crew. On one occasion he went into a detailed explanation of how to clean and paint the *San Francisco* because "I do not approve of the manner painting is done and paint work is treated." He constantly harassed his commanders about coal consumption. Although the regulation requiring the amount of coal used to be recorded in the ship's log had been abolished years before, Selfridge demanded daily coal reports, including explanations for the quantity expended.

After retiring, Selfridge lived in Washington, D.C. He died there on February 4, 1924, at the age of eighty-eight. Selfridge was an intelligent and gifted officer who rose to the height of his profession. His contemporaries quite early recognized his unusually intense ambition, or what Admiral Porter called his "search for fame." He more than likely was aided in his professional ambitions by important connections, particularly the fact that he was the son of a ranking officer in the Navy. Nevertheless, it was not this but his courage, leadership, and seamanship that earned him respect from his peers and superiors.

Selfridge's *Memoirs* were originally published in 1924. The introduction was written by Captain Dudley W. Knox, U.S.N. (Ret.), later the first Director of Naval History. Captain Knox in his remarks stressed the contribution that the *Memoirs* would make on the naval profession. "Young or old," he wrote, "no American naval officer can afford not to read this autobiography...." Knox also hoped that "the younger generation of Americans" would profit by reading this account of a career "which typifies that deep-rooted naval tradition underlying high esprit and efficiency."

The book generally received good reviews in the press. The *New York World* observed that "The *Memoirs* of Thomas O. Selfridge, Jr. contains the salient events in the life of an American Rear Admiral who is the embodiment of the old navy man." The *Literary Review* wrote that the autobiography was "a simple, direct, unaffected personal narrative of a finely lived life, full of achievement." Yet, the major historical journals ignored it. Neither the *Mississippi Valley Historical Review* (now the *Journal of American History*), nor the *American Historical Review* carried reviews of it. This can at least be partly explained that by the mid-1920s there was little interest in military affairs in the history profession.

It was not until the centennial years of the Civil War that the value of the *Memoirs* was recognized by historians. A number of naval histories published during those years (Bern Anderson, *By Sea and by River*; Virgil C. Jones, *The Civil War at Sea*; James M. Merrill, *The Rebel Shore*; John G. Milligan, *Gunboats Down the Mississippi*, and others) all cited Selfridge's *Memoirs*. Since then, works published on the naval aspects of the war have continued to utilize it.

The autobiography is generally well written, factual, and at times absorbing reading. His description of the Battle in Hampton Roads is colorful. Selfridge recognized the attraction of the *Monitor* to the public even then, and although his command of this famous warship was brief, he went into more detail about this ship than any other episode in his life. The book is weighed heavily towards the Civil War; very little, for example, is written about his command of the European Squadron which should have been the high water mark of his career. The book leaves the reader with the impression that Selfridge was as Captain Knox wrote, an officer "who embod[ied] all the finest traditions of our Navy."

BIBLIOGRAPHY

There are a number of brief sketches of Selfridge. *The National Cyclopedia of American Biography*, *The Dictionary of American Biography*, and W. N. Powell and Edward Shippen, *Officers of the Army and Navy (Regular) Who Served in the Civil War* (Philadelphia, 1892) include biographies of Selfridge. See also, Eugene Didier, "The Active Rear Admirals of the United States Navy," *Chautauguan*, XXIV (February, 1897), 569–76; Lewis R. Hamersly, *Records of Living Officers of the U.S. Navy* (Philadelphia, 1894); "Thomas O. Selfridge, Jr." *United Service*, New Series, VII (May, 1892). 529–30; Clark Reynolds, "Thomas O. Selfridge, Jr.," in *Famous Admirals* (New York, 1978).

In addition to the *Memoirs*, Selfridge wrote several articles: "The *Cumberland*," District of Columbia Commandery, Military Order of the Loyal Legion of the United States, *War Papers*, no. 67 (Washington, 1907); "The *Merrimac* and the *Cumberland*," *Cosmopolitan*, XV (June, 1893), 176–84; "The Navy at Fort Fisher," in *Battles and Leaders of the Civil War*, Robert U. Johnson and Clarence C. Buell (eds.) (4 vols., New York, 1956 edition), IV, 362–65. There is also an extensive collection of Selfridge papers in the Naval Historical Foundation, Manuscript Division, Library of Congress.

For additional information on Selfridge, see

Bibliography

Edwin C. Bearss, *Hardluck Ironclad: The Sinking and Salvage of the Cairo* (Baton Rouge, 1966); Park Benjamin, *The United States Naval Academy* (New York, 1900); James L. Christley, "The Alligator," *Civil War Times Illustrated*, XIX (February, 1981), 26–31; Kenneth J. Hagan, *American Gunboat Diplomacy and the Old Navy 1877–1889* (Westport, Conn., 1973); Peter Karsten, *The Naval Aristocracy* (New York, 1972); Clarence MacCartney, *Mr. Lincoln's Admirals* (New York, 1956); G. Mark, *The Land Divided: A History of the Panama Canal and other Isthmian Canal Projects* (New York, 1944); Sophie P. De Meissner, *Old Naval Days* (New York, 1920); John D. Milligan, *Gunboats Down the Mississippi* (Annapolis, 1965); Milton F. Perry, *Infernal Machines: The Story of Confederate Submarines and Mine Warfare* (Baton Rouge, 1965); David D. Porter, *Incidents and Anecdotes of the Civil War* (New York, 1885); Winfield Scott Schley, *Forty-Five Years Under the Flag* (New York, 1904); James R. Soley, *Historical Sketch of the United States Naval Academy* (Washington, D.C., 1876); William N. Still, Jr., *American Sea Power in the Old World* (Westport, Conn., 1980); Richard S. West, Jr., *The Second Admiral: A Life of David Dixon Porter, 1813–1891* (New York, 1937).

Memoirs of Admiral Selfridge

Memoirs of Admiral Selfridge

CHAPTER I

GENEALOGY AND ENTRY INTO NAVY

NOTWITHSTANDING a belief that the writing of memoirs has been overdone, the authors too often having little to say of more than passing interest to anyone but themselves, I have been persuaded by my wife and friends to set down the principal incidents of my long naval career. Their kindly contention is that such a chronicle will preserve data of interest to my children, and of historical value, and I hope they may not be too far wrong.

Since the character and capacity, and consequently the actions, of men are necessarily in large degree products of inheritance, at least a brief genealogical reference should not be omitted herein.

My great-great-grandfather, Edward A. Selfridge, was a native of Scotland, which he left for Ireland, from a reluctance to join the Stuart rebellion against Cromwell, in the early part of the eighteenth century. Not liking Ireland, he emigrated thence to America with his wife, Elizabeth Burns, a relative of the far-famed poet of that name. They settled in Worcester County, Massachusetts, where their son Edward Selfridge was born.

Edward became a thrifty and common-sense farmer of Hubbardston, Massachusetts. His eldest son, Thomas Oliver Selfridge, was born there in February, 1775.

My grandfather, Thomas Oliver Selfridge, evinced a love of literature and a dislike for farming, and these tastes prompted his father to prepare him for college. He entered Harvard College in 1797, graduated in 1801, and after taking up the study of law, entered upon the practice of that profession in Boston in 1803. From the start he was successful as a lawyer and had a brilliant career before him, but unfortunately these favorable prospects were terminated by an early death in 1815, when he was but 41 years old.

In politics he was of the Hamiltonian School. He went with his party so long as he considered it acted in accordance with his views of right and wrong; but no longer. In common with many of his political friends, he disapproved of the opposition of the great body of the Federal party in New England, to the general government, after the declaration of war with Great Britain in 1812. This opposition finally led to a secession from party ranks by the New England Federalists.

Mr. Selfridge was a warm friend of the Navy, when it had but few supporters in the northern section of the country before Hull's victory. He wrote for it, associated with and entertained its officers, rejoiced in its successes, and equally deplored its reverses.

My grandfather had five children, all boys, two of whom died in infancy. The others were Edward A. Selfridge, Thomas Oliver Selfridge (my father), and Christopher G. Selfridge.

Deprived of a father's care at an early age, my uncle Edward shipped before the mast and made a voyage to the northwest coast of America. He rose rapidly and at nineteen commanded a merchant ship which sailed from Boston for Antwerp, with specie to purchase a homeward cargo. Two days out, the crew mutinied, killed Captain Selfridge and his mate, and compelled the steward, the only person remaining who understood navigation, to take the vessel to Halifax. From there the mutineers hoped to get away with the specie, but being apprehended, they were afterwards hung in Boston for piracy.

My uncle Christopher became a Naval Constructor, and in 1855 died of yellow fever at Pensacola, Florida.

My grandfather's friends obtained a warrant as Midshipman for my father, Thomas Oliver Selfridge, who entered the Navy in January, 1818, at the age of twelve years. His first service was on the *Independence,* bearing the flag of Commodore William Bainbridge. He was next detailed to the line of battle ship *Columbus,* and after a cruise in the Mediterranean, was ordered to the *Delaware,* a seventy-four, which served on the same station.

On returning to the United States, my father was ordered before a Board of Examination for promotion to Lieutenant, and passed number two of his date. At this period the Navy was so much reduced in force that it was difficult for officers to get details for sea duty. Accepting the situation, and not wishing to be idle, but to improve his seamanship, he joined the *Union,* an East Indiaman, and as third mate made one voyage to China and return. Afterwards he made voyages as second and first mates in Boston ships to Russia and the West Indies. His "owners" wished him to remain in the merchant service, and offered him the command of a fine ship, but he preferred service in the Navy, which he rejoined.

Then came a second period of duty on the *Delaware,* a cruise on the frigate *United States* in the Mediterranean, service on the frigate *Hudson* on the Brazil Station, and duty on the sloop-of-war *Natchez* on the West Indies Station. In 1838 he was ordered as First Lieutenant of the *North Carolina,* flagship of. the Pacific Squadron. Her captain having been sent home on account of illness, my father was practically the commander of the *North Carolina* during her whole cruise. While so acting he performed a fine piece of seamanship in raising the armed schooner *Shark*, which had been capsized in the harbor of Callao.

After various shore assignments, he sailed for the China Station as commander of the *Columbus*, seventy-four. When war broke out with Mexico the ship left China for the west coast of America, where Captain Selfridge was detached and ordered to command the sloop-of-war *Dale*. In an attack on Guaymas, while ashore in command of the *Dale's* landing force, he was severely wounded, and being incapacitated for duty was sent home on a little barque called the *Whitton*. In so small a vessel he suffered much from his wound, especially in the rough weather encountered while rounding Cape Horn.

Upon the breaking out of the Civil War Captain Selfridge was ordered to the command of the steam frigate *Mississippi,* attached to the Gulf Squadron. He was afterwards Commandant of the Mare Island Navy Yard, and then of the Philadelphia Navy Yard. He retired upon completion of this, his last duty, and in October, 1903, died at the age of ninety-eight years; one of the oldest, if not the very oldest, officers ever carried on the Navy List.

Having a natural aptitude for the sea, my father's schooling in the merchant marine, and a long experience in naval vessels of all types, made him a master of detail and a thorough seaman. An old naval captain told me that my father had no superiors in the Navy as a seaman; being able not only to rig a ship, but to construct one. He pursued the study of naval architecture for many years, and so mastered the subject that he could both draft the lines of a ship and make the intricate calculations also.

My father designed many models of war vessels and they received high praise from critics, but the jealousy of the Bureau of Construction prevented him the satisfaction of having a ship built upon his designs. A hollow floor, which is a characteristic of the old French designs, and an equal displacement of the fore and after bodies, were the main features of his plans. Many small boats were built after his model, and obtained universal praise for great carrying capacity and stability in a seaway, from officers who handled them.

Born February 6, 1836, in Charlestown, Mass., my own naval education may be said to have begun soon after emerging from the cradle. The association with my father and his friends, and the pronounced naval environment in which we lived, all contributed to give me not only an ambition to enter the Navy, but also an almost instinctive knowledge of rudimentary naval matters. The handicap of frequent changes of schools, incident to the itinerant naval life of my father, was partly compensated by the excellence of the English High School (Boston) which I attended the year before admission to the Naval Academy in 1851.

The Academy had been recently reorganized. Before 1850 it was little more than a finishing school with a short course of one year for young officers who had already served for several years afloat. The novel plan of entering young men who had had no previous naval service, and of occupying them with a four year course of study preliminary to regular service, began in 1850. But the general shortage of officers existing in the Navy at that time caused this class to be sent to sea after completing only one year of the newly prescribed curriculum. Thus my class—in those days designated as "51 date"—succeeded to the honor of being the pioneer class under the present system.

It was many years before the Navy thought well of this method of educating young officers. Especially during my early service, the innovation of giving midshipmen a four years academic course before regular service afloat, was the subject of much general ridicule. "Too much book learning at the expense of practical experience" was the principal substance of the criticism. Until the Civil War, the products of the previous system were habitually scornful of those who held Naval Academy diplomas. But as time went on and the value was demonstrated of the long preliminary academic course, which actually included much practical work also, the attitude of the Navy was reversed. Those who had merely taken the short finishing course in the days before 1851 were then sometimes tempted to proclaim themselves Naval Academy graduates.

The "51 date" was scheduled to graduate in 1855. But the demand for more officers afloat led to the separation of the eleven best students into an advanced class for graduation in 1854; provided they could complete the prescribed course of studies. Five of the eleven failed to keep up with the accelerated pace and dropped back into their original class. I was duly graduated in 1854 at the head of the remaining six, and therefore can justly claim the distinction of being the pioneer graduate of the U. S. Naval Academy.

CHAPTER II

Soon after graduating from the Academy in June, 1854, "Midshipman Selfridge," with two others of the "51 date," reported on board the United States razee *Independence* then at New York preparing for a cruise to the Pacific Station. Captain Tattnall commanded the ship, which flew the broad pennant of Commodore William Mervine. It is an interesting coincidence that my father's first active service was also on the *Independence*. The next two years were to be spent in a cruise around the Horn to California, and thence to Hawaii, Samoa, Chile, and Panama.

Of course the three midshipmen were assigned to the steerage and the six "Passed Midshipmen" already on board invited us to join their mess. The outlay needed for a stock of provisions and equipment amounted to about $100 apiece, to meet which we drew four months' advance pay (about $132), known as "dead horse." The mess lived well during the 54 day passage to Rio, but the day before reaching port our caterer announced a shortage of provisions, there being sufficient only for one more day. Thus we were confronted with a serious financial crisis.

The pay of the six senior midshipmen (or "Passed Midshipmen") was about double that of the three juniors. While they might afford to continue such high living, we had little choice than to withdraw from their mess and form a separate one of our own; limiting our future fare to the regular Navy ration, consisting principally of hard-tack, "salt horse," and beans; the same as the blue-jackets. Most of the mess equipment purchased in the United States had been broken in the passage, so that in its division our share proved very limited indeed. I especially recall three red finger bowls which seemed to bear a charmed life. They had to serve almost every purpose; even that of soup plates and sugar bowls. We would have had difficulty in avoiding near starvation but for the resourcefulness of "Jim," our negro steward, who seemed to feel a paternal responsibility and whose influence with the ship's cook must have often resulted in the surreptitious transfer of food from the ship's mess to our own.

I was fortunate in my early detail of duty. Captain Tattnall was a gunnery "sharp," and after observing the preliminary gun drills, called all the officers together and expressed himself as dissatisfied with them. He announced a reorganization in which he, himself, would command the quarterdeck battery with Mr. Selfridge as junior officer of that division. Of course he rarely exercised actual command, so that the work of drilling the division fell almost exclusively to me. Naturally this stimulated my best efforts, which were rewarded at a later inspection when the Captain pronounced the quarterdeck division the best drilled in the ship. However, the amusing aspects of a situation which would restrain the Captain from giving other than praise to his own division, did not escape me.

Before leaving Rio, the discovery that the main-yard was rotten, necessitated extensive alterations in the ship's rig. The fore-yard was substituted for the defective main-yard and a spare topsail yard utilized as a fore-yard. Notwithstanding this jury rig we rounded the Horn in the face of the prevailing head winds without great difficulty; due largely to the fine inherent sailing qualities of the old *Independence*. Under favorable circumstances, I have known her to log 12 or 13 knots when off the wind.

After passing Cape Horn we cruised on the west coast of South America for about a year. One night while I was on watch as midshipman of the quarterdeck, the ship running before a good breeze with all sail set including studdingsails, we were startled by a man rushing on deck and jumping overboard. It was poor Lieutenant Mooney who, while under surveillance for insanity, had escaped from the custody of his medical attendants; and all efforts to rescue him failed.

In due course we reached the Mare Island Navy Yard which in those days was a very small establishment. There was but one pier, to which the *Independence* moored while undergoing repairs. California was then in the midst of her early mining boom, and our crew were not immune from the "gold fever." Desertions became so frequent that the Commodore ordered ball cartridges to be supplied to the marine sentries, and three extra loaded rifles to be kept on the quarterdeck under the supervision of the officer of the watch. One day I had orders to proceed with a cutter on some minor duty. She had been dropped down to the gangway ladder, and while I was standing in the gangway engaged in checking off the crew as they manned the boat, a startling incident occurred. Without warning, about thirty or forty men jumped through the gun deck ports into the cutter and shoved off. Manifestly they were bent on desertion. There was no way to catch them except by manning another boat, which would consume considerable time and therefore did not promise success. The officer of the watch, after vainly ordering the deserting boat to return, picked up his three rifles in succession and tried to fire at the boat, but all rifles misfired. Doubtless the charges had been surreptitiously withdrawn. The marine sentry was then ordered to fire and he wounded one man in the leg. Meantime the boat had gone some distance from the ship, and reaching the opposite side of the strait safely, all the men escaped except the one who was wounded.

When repairs were completed the *Independence* proceeded to Honolulu and thence to Samoa. At the latter place occurred a delay of about six weeks, owing to contrary winds; the passage from the harbor through the reef being too narrow to permit beating out. The delay subsequently caused the belief at home that the ship had been lost, but finally she got away and made Valparaiso without special incident.

This mid-Pacific cruise was made with the ship very short of officers. At that period there was an extensive weeding out from the Navy of the unfit, and from time to time several of the older officers on the *Independence* were ordered home for retirement. At first their places were filled by the six "Passed Midshipmen," but some of the latter did not get on well with the Commodore, who successively placed them under suspension, and finally detailed me as a regular watch and division officer. Thus when less than 20 years old I took my turn in the responsible duty of supervising the conduct of affairs on the deck of a large sailing ship where each watch comprised about 250 men.

An experience during a dark night on the Samoa-Valparaiso run made a lasting impression on my memory. We were in the "roaring forties," with the ship logging 12 knots before a strong breeze under single reefed topsails and the foresail.

I had just taken in the mizzen topsail when the Commodore's gong rang. It was answered by a quartermaster named Haley, a fine old-timer who years before had served with my father on the *Columbus* (China Station). From him the Commodore wished to know the state of the weather, and what officer had the deck. When informed on the latter point, the Commodore inquired somewhat confidentially whether Mr. Selfridge was handling the situation satisfactorily. "Oh yes, Sir," replied Haley, "he's all right. He's a chip of the old block, Sir."

On reaching Panama orders were received for me to proceed to Washington for examination for promotion, then conducted by a special board of Admirals. Throughout the cruise my studies had been diligently pursued, so that in the final examination I was able to retain my place at the head of the "51 date." In this the excellent reports of Commodore Mervine were of great service. Among other things, he said that "when Midshipman Selfridge had the deck he felt confident that all would go well." Thus was the rank of "Passed Midshipman" attained. Subsequently I was promoted to the rank of Master in 1858.

CHAPTER III

"NAUTILUS" AND "VINCENNES"

MY first duty as Passed Midshipman (and Acting Master) was on board the schooner *Nautilus*, then engaged in coast-survey work. From New York she proceeded to Chesapeake Bay for a survey of the Rappahannock River. This completed, while the Captain was on leave I took her to New York, preliminary to surveying the Hudson, and upon arrival a minor incident occurred which tickled my young pride. After anchoring near the *Wabash* I went on board that vessel to make a personal call on my brother-in-law, then a passed assistant surgeon. The call completed, request was made upon the officer of the deck, a gray haired lieutenant, if he would be kind enough to have my gig called to the gangway. "Your what?" said the officer of the deck. "My gig, if you please; I am in command of the *Nautilus* and my gig is lying off your quarter." After the gig departed the old lieutenant rather testily enquired of my brother-in-law, "Who in the devil was that young officer who wanted *his gig?*"

Eight or nine months in all were spent on the *Nautilus,* and when but a few miles of the Hudson River survey had been finished, I was transferred to the sloop-of-war *Vincennes.* She soon sailed for the west coast of Africa to cooperate with British vessels in suppressing the slave trade; both nations having agreed by treaty to maintain a certain number of guns on the coast for that purpose. The fast paddle-wheel steamers of the British were naturally more successful than our old sailing vessels. Moreover the British had the incentive of prize money. They established a prize court at St. Helena, through which quick judgments and prompt distribution of prize money were made; whereas any vessels that the Americans might capture would have to be sent to the distant United States. The *Vincennes* chased several slavers, but was unable to come up with them, and her two and one half years of monotony on that coast bore little result.

On one occasion she was becalmed within two miles of a likely prize. Another officer and myself urged the Captain to send a boat to board her, but he said that he knew her to be a certain Salem whaler. As a matter of fact we learned later that she was a slaver, and thus we lost our only real chance for prize money.

At another time while lying at our base at Saint Paul de Lowando, the Captain of H. M. S. *Triton* asked our cooperation in the capture of an

American slaver which was supposed to be due off the mouth of the Congo River to receive a large number of slaves which, in accordance with custom, had been assembled to await delivery. Under the treaty, the British were not permitted to capture American slavers, so that our Captain sent me with a boat and crew to the British vessel, which dropped us at the mouth of the Congo and then left the vicinity. That same afternoon a vessel came in sight and was practically becalmed about ten miles offshore. We had a long and hot pull to her, but found that she was a legitimate whaler. After spending the night on board, through the courtesy of her captain, we returned up river and, constructing a tent out of the boat sails, camped for two days, until the *Vincennes* came for us. It was suspected that our presence was made known to the supposed slaver, but at all events she never appeared.

This cruise was a very unpleasant one on account not only of the climate and the isolation, but also the unsociability, not to say tyranny, of our Captain. All of the ship's officers were constantly harassed by him and often placed under suspension. My principal duty was that of navigator, though frequently it was necessary to take a watch when the other officers were sick.

The memory of one disagreeable task survives to this day. The Navy Regulations required that the master of a vessel inspect the rigging each morning. On such a small ship as the *Vincennes* a similar inspection made by the boatswain was quite sufficient to comply with all necessities and the spirit of the Regulations, but the Captain insisted upon the letter. Every morning at 6 o'clock I had to go aloft as far as the topmost head of each mast and make this unnecessary, irksome, and perfunctory inspection.

There was but one break in the monotony of the cruise; a short trip to Madeira. The Captain could have remained there a month, but much to our disappointment, and without apparent reason, he returned to the coast after a few days. We always believed that this decision arose from the Captain's peculiar disposition and lack of associates making him jealous of the good time we were having.

While on the station the ship usually stayed either at Porto Praya, in the Cape Verde Islands, or at Saint Paul de Lowando, on the coast of Africa, about 150 miles south of the Congo River. The former place had originally been the only American base in this region where ships' stores were kept, but it fell to our lot to move these stores to Saint Paul de Lowando and there establish a new base. The only compensation for this laborious move was the discovery of a cask of very fine old whiskey, which had apparently been left by accident among the other stores. We took it on board, bought it, and found it much better than the regular issue of grog.

At Porto Praya I nearly lost my life, through a
fondness for boat sailing. Leaving the ship one
afternoon with a cutter and sailing party in a stiff
trade wind, the boat was capsized, when off a
point of land several miles away, by a sudden
squall, such as are of common occurrence there.
The offshore wind drifted us rapidly seawards,
and in spite of all endeavors we could not right
the boat; held on her side by the masts and sails.
In this condition, with an overturned boat that we
could but lightly touch from lack of buoyancy,
surrounded by large man-eating sharks, drifting
under a strong wind to sea, our plight was desperate. Fortunately the officers of the *Vincennes,*
alarmed over our non-appearance, sent out a cutter
which after some hours found the upturned boat
and saved our lives.

One of the interesting aspects of this cruise on
the *Vincennes,* more than 60 years ago, was the
difficulty of maintaining a supply of fresh water.
In this mechanical age it is hard to realize that the
old sailing ships had no distilling plants, and
wholly depended upon the water that could be carried in their iron tanks. These filled the holds,
accurately fitted to the interior form of the hull,
and to prevent accidental contamination by sea
water, had their manholes caulked, except when
empty. The limited supply, and the ever present
possibility of an unduly long voyage, due to calms,
head winds, or bad weather, made it always neces-

sary to exercise extreme care in expending fresh water. The daily allowance was one gallon to each officer for washing and cooking, and one half gallon to each enlisted man for drinking and cooking. Drinking water was obtained by the crew from a cask ("scuttle butt"), continuously guarded by a marine sentry, from which there was no limit to the quantity drunk, but no water could be carried away. An additional allowance of boiling water for tea and coffee was served out by the ship's cook, who was required to be so economical of cooking water that salt-water had to be used for boiling salt beef and pork in the coppers.

Of course in the large seaports of America and Europe, water was delivered alongside on order by specially built water-boats, so that the replenishment of ship's tanks was comparatively easy. But on the coast of Africa the resupply of the precious fluid was a very laborious undertaking. Casks had to be towed ashore by the ship's pulling boats, filled from some small stream, towed back to the ship, hoisted aboard, and finally discharged into the tanks in the hold, through the starting tub rigged over the fore hatch. The hot climate and surf-bound coast made the task of watering ship exceedingly trying for white men, and it was therefore the custom for each man-of-war to carry a number of natives, so long as she remained on the coast, to perform this and other boat duties.

These blacks were enlisted from a tribe of fisher-

men known as Kroomen, found between Sierra
Leone and Cape Palmas, who also worked on the
beaches for trading vessels. They were of fine
physique, being able to pull an oar all day in the
hot sun without apparent fatigue, and were most
apt in the handling of boats. They were regularly
enlisted for the cruise, and borne on the purser's
books under all sorts of fantastic names; such as
*Sea Breeze, Tom Dollar, Jack Ropeyarn, John
Peasoup,* etc. At the regular Sunday function of
mustering the crew around the capstan, each man
answering to his name as called, the Kroomen came
last, always very proud and smiling as they
answered to their absurd names.

They were an invaluable aid to us and especially
liked the strenuous task of getting water; for they
felt at home rolling the filled casks from the watering place, fastening them together with a line, and
laboriously towing them back to the ship with the
boats. Before sailing for home, we paid off and
left our good-natured Kroomen at Monrovia, the
port where they had been enlisted.

At the end of two and one half years we were
overjoyed to receive orders to Boston. The passage home was unduly delayed by heavy westerly
weather, and the Captain, being somewhat timid,
had unbent the royals and stowed them below
before making the American coast. Finally Cape
Cod was sighted and a pilot picked up. His first
remark was, "I expect strong northeast winds to

follow this southwest weather. You had best put on all sail you can. Please set the royals." The Captain replied, "The royals—they have not been set for months and are now down in the hold." Amusement at the Captain's discomfiture repaid us for the hard work of breaking out and setting these sails; and doubly so when the wind came out strong northeast, just after dropping anchor in Boston harbor.

This cruise was the most unpleasant one of my experience. We were all so incensed at the behavior of the Captain that official complaint was made, which resulted in his court martial for tyranny, and, to the best of my recollection, his subsequent punishment in the form of a reprimand.

CHAPTER IV

THE EVE OF WAR

DETACHMENT from the *Vincennes* in the Spring of 1860 was followed by five months sick leave on account of my eyes, which had become strained by constant use in tropical navigation. The rest restored their normal condition and enabled me to pass the examination for promotion to Lieutenant, at the early age of 24 years. The rapidity of my promotion was a result of the extensive weeding out of officers in 1855, when about one hundred and fifty had been retired or otherwise separated from active service.

In September of 1860 I was ordered to the *Cumberland,* Captain Marston commanding. This fine frigate flew the broad pennant of Commodore Pendergrast, commanding the Home Squadron, which then included the entire naval forces of our Atlantic and Gulf coasts. The ship soon sailed for Vera Cruz, where several months were spent in the usual anchorage for large vessels, several miles below the city, without special incident except an occasional "norther." When these severe storms broke, lower yards, light yards, and top gallant-masts were sent down, and the topmasts housed, leaving the ship very bare aloft.

The secession of South Carolina brought the *Cumberland* north, and she arrived in Hampton Roads in March, 1861, shortly thereafter proceeding to the Navy Yard at Norfolk for repairs. The next few weeks were a very anxious time. Naval officers with Southern sympathies, both ashore and afloat, were resigning or preparing to do so, preliminary to going with their States. Virginia had not yet seceded, but a convention in Richmond was considering what action the State should take. The civil population about Norfolk were very much excited, and the more radical among them organized a vigilant committee and made active preparations for hostilities. Virtually all the subordinates of Commodore McCauley in command of the Navy Yard, the senior naval officer present, were Southern officers whose loyalty was doubtful; which fact combined with the Commodore's advanced age, and the practical severance of communications with Washington, tended to make him timid. He was reluctant to adopt any active measures which might possibly be construed as overt acts, and thus possibly influence the convention at Richmond to decide in favor of secession.

At first the *Cumberland* was anchored off the Naval Hospital, where she commanded the approaches to the city, but within a few days, on the advice of Commodore McCauley's pro-Southern officers, she was moved to a berth off the Navy Yard higher up the river. We soon learned that the vigilant committee was blocking the channel to Chesapeake Bay by sinking obstructions off Sewell's Point, about ten miles from the city. Of course their object was to prevent the *Cumberland* and other large vessels present from going out or being reinforced. I volunteered to take the brig-of-war *Dolphin,* then lying at the yard out of commission, with a crew from the *Cumberland,* tow her with the ship's boats to Craney Island and prevent the further sinking of obstructions. Captain Marston and Commodore Pendergrast both thought this an excellent plan and proposed it to Commodore McCauley, who gave his consent. Subsequently, however, the Southern officers prevailed upon him to change the order, maintaining that the youth of Lieutenant Selfridge was likely to result in such rashness as might precipitate a crisis which would throw Virginia to the Confederacy. Had my plan been adopted, the powerful steam frigate *Merrimac,* then lying at the Yard and which afterwards destroyed the *Cumberland* as well as other valuable vessels, could have been saved, if not the Yard itself.

A few days later our lookout at the masthead observed the construction of earthworks on the opposite shore just below the Navy Yard, at a position where the mounting of a battery would command the Yard and its approaches from seaward. Both the Commodore and the Captain being away from the ship, the executive officer sent me ashore to report the situation to Commodore McCauley, who was much perturbed at the news and asked my opinion of what should be done. I recommended that he send me with a flag of truce to Norfolk; there to inform the commanding general that if the work of mounting batteries continued, the *Cumberland* and other vessels present would fire on the city. Commodore McCauley liked this plan and directed that it be carried out.

About an hour later I landed at Norfolk under a flag of truce which fortunately was respected by the large and excited crowd collected on the water-front. Captain Pegram, who had but recently resigned his commission as commander in the Navy, and was then acting as a kind of provost marshal of the city, took me to the headquarters of the commanding general, a State militia officer. On delivering my message to him in very forcible terms, he objected that it would be a terrible thing to fire upon such an undefended city. The reply was that it would also be a terrible thing if batteries were erected and the Yard and men-of-war present were destroyed. Finally the interview was terminated by sending Colonel Heth, who later became a rather prominent Confederate general, to go with me to Commodore McCauley and discuss the matter.

During the subsequent visit upon the Commodore, Colonel Heth spent much time in discussing a variety of matters, but refrained from bringing up the question of the earthworks. I took no part in the conversation, having withdrawn a little distance, until it became apparent that the Colonel was avoiding the main issue. Then asking Commodore McCauley for a word with him confidentially, I again emphasized the need of stopping the work upon the batteries; whereupon he succeeded in obtaining effective assurances from Colonel Heth that the work would cease.

Another incident of those anxious days had a more amusing aspect. A line of small river steamers regularly plied between Norfolk and the Dismal Swamp district, and much to our rage their crews habitually blackguarded us as they passed close to the *Cumberland.* At my suggestion, just at dusk the Captain permitted a 5″ or 6″ hawser to be run across the channel from the ship to the shore and hauled taut. As the evening steamer later approached from Norfolk, the *Cumberland's* rail and ports were crowded with an eagerly expectant company, which indulged in a great cheer when the invisible hawser swept over the steamer, carrying away miscellaneous top hamper, including even the smokestack. This lesson was sufficient to stop any further annoyance from them.

Soon after the capture of Fort Sumter on April 12th, Commodore McCauley received news of the arrival of numerous Confederate troops at Norfolk and Portsmouth. He gave orders to destroy property at the Navy Yard which might be useful to the Confederacy should it become necessary to abandon the Yard. I was sent ashore to do this work. It seemed an impossible task with my small force of only a few boat crews, and we were compelled to limit the work to the spiking of a number of guns, and other minor measures short of setting fire to property. The *Germantown,* lying at the Yard out of commission, happened to be berthed under the big sheer-legs. We pulled out the main supporting pin of those legs and allowed them to drop on the ship, with the result that her masts and hull were badly shattered. It was difficult to decide what to do with the *Merrimac,* a very large, fine vessel of the most modern type, with repairs almost completed. In fact she actually had steam up, her dock trials having just been finished. While no guns were yet mounted, their installation could have been quickly and easily accomplished. I had previously suggested putting some men from the *Cumberland* on board, getting a volunteer crew of firemen from among the Navy Yard workmen, and taking her out; but Commodore McCauley disapproved this plan, fearing that it might be considered as an overt act.

Orders were received to sink her by opening the sea valves, which to me seemed a great pity. I represented to Captain Marston that she should be left afloat so long as there remained a possibility of our being able to take her out; that any imperative need of sinking her quickly could be met by several rounds from our pivot guns, only a few yards distant; and that such method would effectively prevent an easy salvage by the Confederates, which the opening of sea valves would not do even if she was subsequently burned. Later events proved the wisdom of this counsel which did not prevail. The orders were carried out and the *Merrimac* slowly sank until she grounded, with her gun deck a little above water.

Rumors had reached us that a steamer was to come from Richmond carrying a large number of soldiers to board and take the *Cumberland* by surprise. Naturally we were on the alert to prevent this, each night maintaining a full watch at the guns, and rigging the boarding nettings; large nets spread between the lower yardarms and the rail on each side. At about 8 P.M. on the same day that the *Merrimac* had been scuttled, the drums unexpectedly beat to quarters, and I rushed to my 10-inch pivot gun on the forecastle. We could make out a large steamer standing towards us from seaward. It was manifestly important that, if hostile, she should not be allowed to approach too near, since otherwise we might be boarded before sufficient gunfire could be directed against her. I had laid the pivot gun towards her and taken the lock string myself, for fear that the gun captain might misfire from excitement. Finally, when no answer was received to our several hails, I sang out to the Captain, "Shall I fire, Sir?" He replied "No, we will hail her once more." This was done and from the Receiving Ship *Pennsylvania,* lying just below us, came the reply "Do not fire, it is the *Pawnee.*" A moment more and a ten-inch shell would have swept decks crowded with soldiers.

The *Pawnee* had been sent down from Washington with Commodore Paulding and a number of officers, under orders to evacuate and destroy the Navy Yard immediately, after taking out certain ships of special fighting value, which of course included the *Cumberland* and the *Merrimac.* Then the folly of so much previous destruction became clearly evident; to raise the *Merrimac,* and place her machinery again in condition, or to repair the *Germantown* and other useful ships which had been damaged, would consume several days, at least. Commodore Paulding considered it urgent that the evacuation begin at once, so as to minimize the risk of the *Cumberland* and *Pawnee* being blocked in by any further obstruction of the lower channel, and he gave orders to apply the torch to the large buildings ashore and to all the ships that might be of value to the enemy.

I thought at the time, and have had no reason to change my opinion, that the evacuation and partial destruction which followed was an irretrievable blunder, brought about by the paralyzing effort of the authorities at Washington, in their abortive attempt to keep the border States in the Union. I do not hesitate to state that the Yard could have been held by the *Cumberland* and *Pawnee,* which had 100 Marines and a regiment of Massachusetts volunteers on board, until the ordnance stores and the *Merrimac* could have been removed or effectively destroyed, if not longer. Meantime the channel could have been easily guarded against further blocking, by manning and employing some of the smaller vessels present.

The sequel to abandoning the *Merrimac* is common knowledge; but it is not so generally known that a vast quantity of ammunition and naval stores, and 3,000 guns of all calibers, most of them uninjured, were also left for the uses of the Confederacy, whose facilities for the manufacture of munitions were extremely limited. But for this supply, and the workshops of the Yard, the rebels would have had great difficulty in conducting the war, especially in its early stages. Some of these guns were quickly mounted at Sewell's Point, Hatteras Inlet, and other points along the coasts which served blockade runners so well. The guns of the strong fortifications at Gloucester Point, York River, which prevented the Confederate line at Yorktown from being flanked and caused McClellan to lose a precious month in the attempt to reduce it, were from the Norfolk Yard. Guns from the same place were subsequently encountered at Forts Henry and Donelson, Island No. 10, Memphis, Vicksburg, Grand Gulf, Port Hudson, Fort De Russy, and even well up the Red River.

A few hours after the order was given to apply the torch, there was a magnificent, if melancholy and depressing spectacle. One fourth of the whole Federal Navy, including two of its biggest ships, and its largest naval base, were in flames. Among the large vessels, the old frigate *United States* was the only one spared; we could not bear to destroy such an embodiment of naval tradition.

At 4 A. M., just before the fires of destruction were begun, the *Cumberland* cast off her moorings and stood out in tow of the small steamer *Yankee,* preceded down channel by the *Pawnee.* The scene was most impressive. The great conflagration made it as light as day. Norfolk was in the hands of an armed mob, which lined the shores, angry at the destruction which was taking place. As the *Cumberland* passed, both batteries were well manned, prepared at the first fire from shore to pour in her broadsides. But they refrained from attacking us, and we had no adventure until nearly ten miles beyond, where at daylight the *Cumberland* was brought up on the channel obstructions, the placing of which I had endeavored so hard to prevent. After several hours, with the assistance of the *Pawnee, Yankee,* and the *Keystone State,* sent from Old Point, the obstructions were crushed by the weight of the ship being dragged over them, and we proceeded to an anchorage off Fortress Monroe.

CHAPTER V

THE FIRST SKIRMISHES

Soon after the evacuation of Norfolk, an incident occurred which led to my first shot of the war and the receipt of my first prize money. A number of local craft were anchored inside of Hampton Bar. One morning a tug took two of these in tow and started in the direction of Norfolk. Not having any steam craft immediately available, we could not pursue, so I suggested to the Captain that we heave her to by a shot from the forward pivot gun. Aim was taken with great care at about 3,000 yards range, but the shot struck a little short. It ricocheted however and grazed the deck of the tug, doing only slight damage, but greatly alarming the crew, who hastily waved a tablecloth for a flag of truce and hove to. We then sent a cutter, boarded her, and found that the tows were loaded with gun carriages. Several years later, principally on account of the interest attached to the first shot being so lucky, I spun this yarn to Mr. Gideon Welles, Secretary of the Navy. He asked if any prize money had been received, and on my replying in the negative, said that he would refer the case to the Prize Court in Boston. The latter decided in our favor, and out of a total of about $7,500 allowed, my share was $125; a liberal reward for this lucky shot; my first of the war.

While the *Cumberland* lay off Old Point Comfort guarding the approaches to the Elizabeth and James Rivers, I was kept very active on reconnaissance duty, in command of the *Yankee,* a fast light-draft tug. Between April 29th and May 7th, five separate expeditions were made to gain information of possible enemy activity along the shore from Sewell's Point to Cape Henry, and from the mouth of the James River to Gloucester Point, twenty miles up the York River.

Nothing was discovered except small cavalry parties five miles inside of Cape Henry, and the construction of earthworks on Gloucester Point. The latter was first noted on May 6th. A further examination was made the next day, and upon approaching within about 2,000 yards, a shot across our bow first apprised us that the enemy had guns mounted. Continuing to steam slowly ahead, a second shot was fired at us and fell in line, but a little short. The *Yankee's* engines were then stopped, all heavy articles moved to the port side and water pumped from the starboard tanks, as the ship had a considerable list to starboard, due to moving her two guns to that side. We fired

four round shot and two shell at extreme elevation, but all fell short. Meantime the enemy continued firing, two of their shells passing about ten
feet over and bursting twenty yards beyond the
ship. The remainder of their total of twelve
shell fell short. As nearly as could be estimated,
the enemy were using one 8-inch gun and two long
32-pounders, opposed to the *Yankee's* two light 32-
pounders. Such a superiority against us, in
both range and caliber, seemed to render a continu-
ation of the action futile and unwise, after the mission of gaining a good estimate of their strength
had been accomplished. Nevertheless it was with
no little reluctance that I retreated from this, my
first experience under fire; no damage having been
sustained by either side.

After this reconnaissance the *Yankee* was
ordered to Philadelphia for repairs. The return
to Hampton Roads was just in time for me to rejoin the *Cumberland* before her departure for Boston, where the copper sheathing, which had been
badly damaged in forcing her over the obstructions
near Craney Island, was to be repaired in dock.

During our stay at Boston the naval career of
the present Rear Admiral Charles F. O'Neil
began. His family lived at Roxbury and were
friends of my uncle. Young O'Neil had made one
passage as a boy to China and return in a merchant
ship, so that he was a good sailor, and when his
father suggested entering him in the Navy, I laid

the case before Captain Marston. The latter was able to give O'Neil an appointment as Acting Master's Mate, subject to the subsequent approval of the Department, and consequently the lad was one of those who later fought so bravely in the *Cumberland's* historic engagement with the *Merrimac.*

The repairs completed and vacancies in the complement filled, the *Cumberland* rejoined the fleet at Hampton Roads and soon afterward was employed in the blockade of Hatteras Inlet. Since Federal naval forces controlled the lower Chesapeake, Norfolk's main line of water communication was via the Sounds of North Carolina, to which sea access was afforded through this inlet; and there the Confederates had erected two forts, the capture of which was undertaken by the *Cumberland, Minnesota* (flagship of Commodore Stringham), *Pawnee, Susquehanna, Wabash,* and *Monticello* on August 28, 1861. The initial bombardment caused an early evacuation of the outermost fort, with little damage to the fleet, but the second fort, further inside, was more difficult to deal with, since only our larger guns could reach it, and at the end of the first day its flag was still flying.

That night the *Cumberland,* not having any steam power, stood offshore as a precaution against the threatening weather, and was therefore late in joining in the bombardment on the following morning. Standing in under all sail for the line of engaged ships, and luffing ahead of the leading one, we executed a simultaneous evolution of shortening and furling sail, dropping anchor, and opening fire; which the Captain had adopted at my suggestion. It was a very smart and inspiring piece of seamanship, demonstrating the splendid qualities of our crew. Old officers who saw the maneuver have often spoken of the magnificence and beauty of the ship on this, the last occasion of an American frigate going into battle under sail.

The fleet spent most of the forenoon in bombarding the second fort, with little apparent result. Neither did the enemy's return fire do any appreciable damage. Finally a shell from the fleet dropped close over the earthworks and into the ventilator of the bomb-proof, where most of the Confederates were sheltered. It did not explode, but fearing that it might do so, they rushed outside and hoisted a flag of truce. This ended the battle. Several days later I had opportunity to go ashore and investigate what kind of a shell had caused the surrender. The *Cumberland* being the only ship of the fleet carrying 10-inch guns, and since both of her 10-inch guns were in my command, it was a source of great personal gratification to find a 10-inch shell in the bomb-proof.

During the afternoon of the second day's fight, the onset of bad weather, with a strong breeze blowing directly toward the shore, placed the *Cumberland* in a rather bad situation. Her departure was an extremely difficult piece of seamanship. The topsail yards were hoisted and their sails loosed and stopped up to the yard with rope yarn; the courses were also loosed and the yards braced sharp up; a hawser was run to the *Susquehanna* and hove taut, giving the ship a favorable sheer. Then as the anchor broke ground, sail was quickly made, the hawser let go, and the ship stood safely off the dangerous lee shore.

Following this battle we returned to Hampton Roads and anchored in the mouth of the James River off Newport News, in company with the *Congress,* to prevent the egress of privateers which were supposed to be fitting out at Richmond. Here we lay all winter, having rather a monotonous though strenuous time, with constant drills calculated to meet every contingency in a possible combat with the *Merrimac,* the news of whose preparation reached us from time to time.

CHAPTER VI

"CUMBERLAND" AND "MERRIMAC"

AFTER the Norfolk Yard was evacuated the Confederates had raised the *Merrimac,* placed her in dry dock, and cut down the upper works even with the berth deck, leaving a freeboard of not more than two feet. Then a low casemate was built upon her sides receding at an angle of about 45 degrees, and extending through about 200 feet of her length amidships. Upon this casemate slabs of iron, 4 inches wide and 2 inches thick, were attached in two layers diagonal to each other, and the whole backed by two feet of oak. In this way her sides, and also the sloping deck forward and abaft the casemate, were heavily armored. In addition she was fitted with a cast-iron ram, projecting three feet from the stem and starting about six feet under water. Notwithstanding all this armor, the relatively great size of the *Merrimac* (300 ft. long, 52 ft. beam, 24 ft. draft, 4,500 tons displacement) permitted the installation of a heavy battery also. She was armed with one 7-inch rifle in the bow, a similar gun aft, and two 6-inch rifles and six 9-inch guns in the broadside.

Opposed to this formidable battery the *Cumberland* mounted only one rifled gun, a 70-pounder Dahlgren at the stern. On the forecastle was a 10-inch pivot smoothbore gun, while the broadside battery below on the gun deck comprised twenty-two 9-inch shell guns. Thus the superiority of her battery alone gave the *Merrimac* a substantial advantage over the *Cumberland;* but when in addition we consider the *Merrimac's* great mobility, due to having steam power, and the tremendous offensive and defensive strength afforded by ram and armor, it is manifest that she completely outmatched us in material qualities.

Of course we were not aware of all these details until after the fight, but we knew in a general way that our possible antagonist was being armored, and we took steps to favor the penetration of her armor, by the *Cumberland's* guns. Solid shot was supplied for our 9-inch guns, their normal charge increased from 10 to 13 pounds of powder, and double breechings provided to stand the increased recoil.

But our greatest advantage lay in the exceptional quality of a model crew, that has never been excelled and perhaps rarely equaled. It had been recruited principally from Boston and vicinity, and few changes beyond those incident to expiration of enlistment had occurred since 1860; notwithstanding many inducements to desert, held out to them by Confederate sympathizers during the trying days at Norfolk. These splendid men were proud of their ship, they felt the mutual dependence upon each other arising from long association, and they had been subject to a discipline which gave them great faith in themselves and in the power of their ship. They really believed themselves invincible, and, indeed, could they have had a fair fight, would have shown themselves to be such. The excellence of this crew was all the more important from the fact that the ship was short of officers and many recent changes had been made in the officer personnel; most of the newcomers being young and inexperienced. Of the original officer complement, only Lieutenant Heywood of the Marine Corps and myself remained on board at the time of the fight.

The winter of 1861-62, spent at Newport News awaiting the appearance of the *Merrimac,* was very cold; and to the hardship of being allowed no fires on board and of having to keep one watch sleeping at the guns each night, was added the irksomeness of enforced idleness except for drills and internal routine. Yet the spirit of officers and men was maintained at a high level. The rumors of the expected presence of the *Merrimac* were so frequent as to become a standing joke with the ship's company; but they finally materialized in a most distressing way.

Saturday the eighth of March was a beautiful spring day, mild, bright, and clear. The *Cumber-*

land was lying at single anchor with her sails loosed
to dry, when at twelve thirty P.M., the writer as
Officer-of-the-Deck, reported that the *Merrimac*
had just hove in sight, a long distance off in the
direction of Norfolk. Owing to the mirage, her
movements were much obscured, and her progress
was so slow that at first it seemed doubtful if she
was really coming out. But surmises were dispelled as the large, low hull came in view abreast
of Craney Island, heading for the mouth of the
Elizabeth River.

Our Captain (William Radford) was temporarily absent on court martial duty at Hampton
Roads.[1] The Executive Officer, Lieutenant
George U. Morris, ordered all hands called. The
sails were promptly furled, and then the quick
beat to "quarters" aroused everyone and warned
that the long-expected occasion had finally come.
More than an hour of doubt followed while the
Merrimac was hidden by a high bluff at the mouth
of the James River. We could not see whether,
after leaving the Elizabeth River, she was proceeding towards the squadron in Hampton Roads or
heading for the anchorage of the *Cumberland* and
Congress off Newport News.

Meantime the *Cumberland* presented an inspir-

---

[1] Upon the appearance of the *Merrimac* in the roads, Captain
Radford hastily procured a horse at Old Point and rode overland
at such a pace, that, on dismounting at Newport News, the horse
dropped dead. He was in time only to see his ship sinking.

ing sight; a splendid type of an old-time frigate; towering masts, long yards, neat and trim man-of-war appearance, with her crew standing at their guns for the last time; cool, grim, silent and determined Yankee seamen, the embodiment of power, grit, and confidence. I firmly believe that the sheer force of their confident determination to conquer would have prevailed over the armor and ram of the *Merrimac,* but for the handicap of sail motive power.

At 2:30 our doubts as to the objective chosen by the *Merrimac* were set at rest by her reappearance from behind the bluff, heading in our direction. As she passed the *Congress,* anchored below us, the latter opened with her whole broadside; but it merely rattled from the sloping armor like hail upon a roof. This effect caused us neither surprise nor shaken confidence in our own powers, since the *Congress* armament could fire nothing to compare with the solid shot of 80 pounds which we could deliver.

Disdaining to reply to her weaker antagonist, the *Merrimac* steamed slowly across the bow of the *Cumberland* and maneuvered for a ramming position. We had much difficulty in bringing any guns to bear. The springs which had been run long before, to provide against this very contingency of having to swing the ship to meet maneuvers of a mobile enemy, now proved useless from the fact of the turn of the tide having swung the *Cumberland* athwart the channel; thus bringing the springs in line with her keel. Three times the gun deck divisions were sent from one battery to the other without gaining any opening, while the head rigging prevented the 10-inch forecastle pivot gun from firing. At last the *Merrimac's* bearing changed sufficiently to starboard to permit our opening fire with a few forward 9-inch guns and the bow pivot gun. The enemy at once replied with her 7-inch rifle and broadside guns, sometimes aiming the latter at the small fort on shore, whose fire could have no material effect upon the action.

The *Merrimac's* first shot passed through the starboard hammock netting, killing and wounding nine marines, and knocking down, but not injuring, their commander, Lieutenant Heywood. These men, the first to fall, were promptly carried below, and their groans were something new to us and served as an introduction to a scene of carnage unparalleled in the war. The *Merrimac* continued to lay about 300 yards sharp on the starboard bow, raking the *Cumberland* with every shot from her broadsides, while we could reply only by extreme train with the few guns already mentioned. It was a situation to shake the highest courage and the best discipline, but our splendid crew never faltered.

Of even the few guns that could bear, No. 1 on the gun deck was fired but once. The second shell from the murderous 7-inch rifle burst among the crew as they were running the gun out, after loading for a second shot, literally destroyed the whole crew except the powder boy, and disabled the gun for the remainder of the action. The captain of this gun, a splendid seaman named Kirker, rated commodore's coxswain, had both arms taken off at the shoulder as he was holding his handspike and guiding the gun. He passed me while being carried below, but not a groan escaped from him.

At this time the spring from the starboard quarter was manned on the spar deck, with the object of bringing the broadside to bear, but for the reasons previously explained the attempt proved futile. Events followed too fast to remember them in detail, during fifteen minutes of the most gruelling punishment. The dead were thrown to the disengaged side of the deck; the wounded carried below. No one flinched, but everyone went on rapidly loading and firing; the places of the killed and wounded being taken promptly by others, in accordance with previous drill and training. The carnage was frightful. Great splinters torn from the ship's side and decks caused more casualities than the enemy's shell. Every first and second captain of the guns of the first division was killed or wounded, and with a box of cannon primers in my pocket, I went from gun to gun firing them as fast as the decimated crews could load.

The *Merrimac* was not satisfied even with the

great advantage of gunfire incident to her raking position. The resistance from the *Cumberland* promised such delay, damage, and expenditure of ammunition as would handicap further operations against the Federal fleet, and Captain Buchanan decided to ram. The *Merrimac* struck the *Cumberland* upon the starboard bow, the ram penetrating the side under the berth deck, and for a few minutes holding the two ships together. As the *Cumberland* commenced to sink, the *Merrimac* was also carried down until her forward deck was under water. This situation presented an opportunity which unfortunately our officers on deck failed to seize. If our anchor had been let go it would have fallen on the *Merrimac's* deck and probably have held the two ships together; thus sinking the *Merrimac* with the *Cumberland.*

But no such action was taken. The ram was broken off in the *Cumberland's* side by the combined strain of the *Cumberland's* sinking and the swinging of the *Merrimac* under the influence of the tide. The current brought her up broadside to us, and whether from demoralization over the narrow escape, engines caught on center, or from some other reason, there she lay for some moments without moving; finally giving the *Cumberland* her first fair opportunity to fight back. That it was quickly and fully exploited regardless of our sinking condition, and notwithstanding the carnage that surrounded us, is sufficient justification for the emphasis which I have placed upon the qualities of that peerless crew.

Three solid broadsides in quick succession were poured into the *Merrimac* at a distance of not more than one hundred yards. Confederate officers have told me that it made her fairly reel. Cheer upon cheer went up from the *Cumberland,* unfortunately only to be followed by exclamations of rage and despair as the enemy slowly moved away. But in spite of her armor she was not unscathed. Noting the small effect of our fire upon her sides, the gun captains had been instructed to aim only at the gun ports, with the result that the muzzles of two of her broadside 9-inch guns had been shot away.

The water was rising rapidly, the *Cumberland* going down by the bows. The forward magazine was flooded, but the powder tanks had been whipped out and carried aft, whence the supply of powder to the forward guns had been subsequently maintained. As the water gained the berth deck, which by this time was filled with the badly wounded, heart-rending cries above the din of combat could be heard from the poor fellows as they realized their helplessness to escape slow death from drowning.

Having reached a position free from our fire the *Merrimac* hailed the *Cumberland* and asked if she would surrender. The reply went back from Lieutenant Morris, "Never! We will sink with our colors flying"; whereupon the enemy resumed her old raking position on our starboard bow and again opened upon the doomed ship. The first cutter was sent with a hawser from the port quarter to a nearby schooner, and another effort made to spring our broadside to bear, but by that time the *Cumberland* was too waterlogged to be moved.

While the foregoing was in progress the writer gathered together the remnants of the first division, some thirty men, and took them forward, with the object of transporting No. 1 gun to the bridle port, in a position where it would bear upon the *Merrimac*. The tackles had been scarcely hooked, when a shell, passing through the starboard bow, burst among them, killing and maiming the greater number. At about this time Master's Mate Harrington had his head shot off, and fell a corpse at my feet, in the act of receiving an order to slip the cable. There were few men left in the first division, which I had commanded for so long. Not a gun's crew could be mustered from the six crews of brave fellows who had gone into action so confident in their ship only three quarters of an hour before. No men ever stood at their guns better than that first gun deck division of the *Cumberland*.

The appearance of the gun deck forward at this time can never be forgotten. It was covered with the dead and wounded and slippery with blood. Some guns were left run in from their last shot;

rammers and sponges, broken and powder-blackened, lay in every direction; the large galley was demolished and its scattered contents added to the general blood-spattered confusion.

Meanwhile the water had been rapidly gaining in spite of the efforts of the after division which had been sent to the pumps. The *Merrimac* must have noted our rapid sinking, but for some reason which I have never understood, unless to give a final *coup de grâce,* she rammed the *Cumberland* a second time, striking her abaft the fore channels but doing no special damage.

By this time, even if there had been a sufficient number of men left, there was no longer any powder to serve the guns of the first division. The writer started aft, and on the way the ship gave a lurch forward, and water commenced pouring in through the bridle ports. Manifestly she was sinking so rapidly that no time could be lost. The order was passed for "every man to look out for himself"; an order never given until the last extremity.

The survivors rushed aft, some up the ladders from the berth and gun decks, others along the spar deck. Fortunately, all the boats had been lowered before the action commenced, and two of the largest were uninjured. Some of the survivors jumped into these boats moored astern, some climbed the rigging, and still others saved themselves on gratings and wooden material from the deck.

In this moment of dire confusion, with the water

closing over the doomed ship, the last gun was fired, sounding her death knell. It was generally believed that this act of heroism was performed by Coxswain Matthew C. Tierney, who had been mortally wounded and who perished in the ship.

I was one of the last to leave the main deck, the water then being up to the main hatch. Turning to the wardroom hatch ladder, almost perpendicular from the ship having a heavy list to port, I found it blocked by our fat drummer, Joselyn, struggling up with his drum. The peril was imminent, and, throwing off coat and sword, I squeezed through a gun port. In doing so, however, the heel of my boot became jammed against the port sill by the gun, which, from a position partially inboard had been slid outboard by the listing of the ship. For a few precious moments it seemed as though I must be carried down with the rapidly sinking ship; but with much difficulty, from a bent position I finally succeeded in wrenching off the boot-heel and thus freeing my foot. Then jumping into the icy water, encumbered by boots and clothing, I swam to the launch astern and was picked up exhausted. Later the drummer was also rescued while using his drum as a life buoy.

Almost immediately the *Cumberland* took one final plunge, bow first and stern high in the air, and settled beneath the waters. With difficulty the boat was shoved clear of the sinking vessel, whose flag, though almost within our reach, was left to wave over the glorious dead who had defended its honor with their lives.

Thus perished the *Cumberland*. No vessel ever fought more splendidly against odds so great that but one result was possible. She fought to the bitter end until the waters closed over her last gun.

Few battles of the war, ashore or afloat, resulted in so large a proportion of casualties on either side. On the day of this desperate fight the crew of the *Cumberland* numbered 299 bluejackets and 33 marines; of whom 80 were killed or drowned, and about 30 wounded saved. Thus the total casualties were more than 33% of those engaged. The brunt of the fight fell upon my division, which lost more than half of its 85 men.

It is not easy to estimate all the damage done to the *Merrimac*. Two of her crew were killed, and numbers wounded, among the latter being Captain Buchanan; an able officer who was a great loss to the Confederacy. The flagstaff and the muzzles of two guns were shot away. Many of the plates on the casemates were loosened. The smokestack was so perforated with shot holes, as to fill the gun deck with smoke and seriously interfere with the working of her battery, and to greatly decrease the draft of the boilers, and hence to lower her speed. Finally the ram was wrenched off in the *Cumberland's* side, causing the *Merrimac* to spring a leak.

Considering the odds against the *Cumberland* there could have been no dishonor in an early surrender. But what would have been the result? Fresh from the surrender, the *Merrimac* would have destroyed the fine frigate *Minnesota,* which had grounded on her way to assist the *Cumberland;* then the capture of the remaining Federal ships in Hampton Roads, consisting of the frigate *Roanoke,* which had lost her screw, and the sailing frigate *St. Lawrence* would have been easily accomplished during the afternoon of March 8th, and the *Monitor* arriving late that night in bad condition after a stormy passage from New York, would have found herself alone.

But for the assistance rendered by the *Minnesota* in getting the *Monitor* ready for action, the latter could not have put up such a good fight as she did on the morning following her arrival. If on this occasion, the *Merrimac's* smokestacks had been intact, the handicap which she suffered of not being able to maneuver as handily as the *Monitor,* would have been much reduced; and when the opportunity to ram presented itself she is likely to have struck the *Monitor* squarely instead of a glancing blow. Moreover if the *Merrimac's* ram had been in place, it is my belief, formed after an inspection of the *Monitor* only a few days later, that even the glancing blow would have sunk the *Monitor.* Therefore I am firmly convinced that the great sacrifice made for the honor of the flag by the crew of the *Cumberland,* though it failed to save their ship, resulted in the much greater achievement of saving the fleet, if not the Union.

History gives no example of braver resistance in the face of utter hopelessness, no precedent of a sterner feeling of "never surrender," than was shown by the *Cumberland* on the 8th of March, 1862. With the steadying influence of but few officers, exposed to a terrible shell fire for the first time in their lives, with little opportunity to fight back, seeing great numbers of their comrades mangled and killed before them, with the rising water pouring over the decks, and the ship trembling in her last throes; the manner in which those decimated guns' crews stood unflinchingly at their quarters until the word was passed from their officers, "Every man look out for himself"; was truly sublime and ought to embalm the name of *Cumberland* in the heart of every American; regardless of the military results accomplished. Without hope of assistance, against fearful odds, those splendid fellows fought to the bitter end, and the ship was their tomb. Let their memory be kept green in the hearts of their countrymen, and if their example stimulates the youth of coming generations to be true to their country and their flag, it cannot be said they died in vain.

"No braver vessel ever flung her pennon to the breeze,
  No bark e'er died a death so grand;
  Her flag the gamest of the game
  Sank proudly with her, not in shame
  But in its ancient glory—

"Cumberland" and "Merrimac"

The memory of its parting gleam
Will never fade while poets dream,
The echo of her dying gun
Will last till man his race has run,
Then live in Angels' history." [1]

[1] The Officers of the *Cumberland* on the 8th of March, 1862, in the fight with the *Merrimac* were:

> Lieut. Geo. U. Morris, Executive Officer.
> Lieut. Thos. O. Selfridge, Jr.
> Master W. S. Stuyvesant.
> Acting Master W. W. Kennison.
> Acting Master W. P. Randall.
> 2nd. Lieut. Marines, Chas. Heywood.
> Surgeon Chas. Martin.
> Asst. Surgeon Edward Kershner.
> Paymaster Cremer Burt, absent.
> Chaplain John T. Lenhart, killed.
> Acting Master's Mate John Harrington, killed.
> Acting Master's Mate Chas. O'Neil.
> Acting Master's Mate H. Tyson.
> Acting Master's Mate H. Wyman.
> Boatswain Edward Bell.
> Gunner Eugene Mack.
> Carpenter W. M. Laighton.
> Sailmaker David Bruce.
> Paymaster's Clerk Hugh Knott.
> Pilot Lewis Smith.

Lieutenant Morris as Executive Officer, in the absence of Captain Radford, was in command. On the gun deck Lieut. Selfridge commanded the forward division of 5 IX-inch guns, Master Stuyvesant the after division of four IX-inch, and the two extreme after guns were manned by Marines.

The guns' crews consisted of sixteen men and a powder boy.

The forward X-inch pivot was in charge of Acting Master Kennison, the after in charge of Acting Master Randall.

Sailmaker Bruce commanded the Powder division assisted by Gunner Mack.

Three soldiers from the shore who had come off to visit the ship were unable to return, and asked permission to join the guns' crews. Two of them were killed, and one escaped.

CHAPTER VII

"MONITOR" AND "MERRIMAC"

AFTER the very distressing loss of the *Cumberland,* the survivors succeeded in landing at Newport News. Furious over the loss of the ship in which I had taken such intense pride, shivering with cold from soaking wet and scanty clothing, the reaction from the long endured, frightful, experiences of battle impelled me to tears, and I sobbed like a child.

The *Merrimac* stood up the river, seeking a wide reach of deep water in which to turn around. Meanwhile the flag of the *Cumberland* was still flying above water at her gaff. We had wanted to rescue it before pulling away from the ship, but at that time it was too high to be reached, since the ship had gone down by the head, lifting her stern well out of the water. Seeing an opportunity to get this flag while the *Merrimac* was up the river, I called for volunteers and pulling off to the ship in a small skiff, took down the flag and returned safely to the shore.

We were met by kind friends in a New York

Zouave Regiment, who took us to the headquarters of Brigadier-General Phelps, where, after hiding the flag in a corner underneath a sofa, an outfit of dry clothing, comprising zouave boots, trousers, and blue shirts, with overcoat, made me more comfortable.

From the shore we observed the *Merrimac* standing down river towards the *Congress,* which vessel slipped her moorings, made sail, and ran aground in shallow water. The *Merrimac* took up a position under her stern and opened a raking fire, to which no reply could be made except with a few guns hastily moved to the stern ports. It was impossible for the *Congress* to keep up such a fight very long, and she surrendered, many of her men, however, jumping overboard and swimming to shore.

Owing to the shallow water the *Merrimac* could not approach very near her prize, so that one of the several tugs which accompanied her was sent in to receive the surrender. Some Indiana infantry opened a rifle fire from shore, and forced the tug to leave the *Congress* before possession had been completed; whereupon the *Merrimac* again resumed fire at the *Congress,* set her on fire, and she was burned.

The Confederate ram then proceeded to attack the *Minnesota,* which had run ashore on the Middle Ground, in trying to come to the assistance of the *Cumberland* and *Congress;* but the great draft of the *Merrimac* prevented her from getting to close quarters, and the lateness of the hour saved the *Minnesota* from destruction.

That evening General Phelps received reports of the approach towards his camp of a rebel column. Preparations were made to repel attack, and to assist in this I gathered together the *Cumberland's* survivors, and marched them out to the defenses. It proved to be a false alarm, and returning to the town I spent the night in the headquarters building, sleeping very soundly after the exhausting day's work. In the morning great was my regret to discover that the *Cumberland's* flag had been taken from its hiding place, and this trophy has never yet been found.

The following day we witnessed from the shore the memorable fight between the *Monitor* and the *Merrimac;* the former having arrived early that morning after a stormy passage from New York, and refitted alongside the grounded *Minnesota.* This duel has been fully described many times and need not be detailed here.

During the afternoon of March 9th, after the *Monitor's* victory, the survivors of the *Cumberland* and *Congress* were sent by tug to the *Roanoke,* then anchored off Old Point and serving as flagship of the senior officer present, Captain Marston. He received us with great kindness and directed that "leave" be granted to all the survivors including myself. Later a message came from Mr. Fox, the Assistant Secretary of the Navy, who had come down from Washington on receipt of news of the *Merrimac* episode, that he wished to see me. Captain Marston had recommended me for the command of the *Monitor* in place of Lieutenant Worden, who had been wounded in the fight, and the Secretary offered me the honor. He emphasized the great trust and responsibility that were involved, saying that the *Monitor* was the only thing between the *Merrimac* and all of the northern cities, and the water communications of our armies. I thanked him for his confidence and replied that, "if the *Merrimac* comes out, the *Monitor* will be on hand."

A few minutes later the officer of the deck of the *Monitor* was amazed to receive a zouave, who had orders to assume command of the vessel. Not wishing to disturb Lieutenant Green, the Executive Officer and acting Captain, from his dinner in the wardroom, I went below, and could scarcely contain my amusement at the surprise of the *Monitor's* officers, upon seeing a zouave back down the narrow hatchway and announce himself as their new commander.

Since it was expected that the *Merrimac* might appear the following morning, the next three hours were spent in making a thorough inspection of the *Monitor,* to familiarize myself, as well as possible at night, with her very novel arrangements. The entire ship was examined, including engine and boiler rooms, turrets and conning tower, and each essential detail was explained to me. The marks where the *Merrimac's* bow had rammed the *Monitor's* side, caused me great gratification, since it was clearly evident that, but for the loss of the *Merrimac's* ram, broken off in the *Cumberland's* side, the *Monitor* would surely have been destroyed. The *Cumberland's* epic fight had not been in vain.

Early next morning, we proceeded to a position off the mouth of the Elizabeth River, and remained without being rewarded by a sight of the *Merrimac*. After four or five days there, Mr. Fox again sent for me and stated that, previous to his having ordered me to command the *Monitor,* he had sent a dispatch boat to Commodore Goldsborough, the Commander-in-Chief of the fleet, who was then off the coast of North Carolina, directing that Lieutenant Jeffers be sent at once to command the *Monitor*. Mr. Jeffers had just arrived and the Secretary was obviously embarrassed at the situation. This was relieved by my pointing out that Lieutenant Jeffers was many years the senior, and that under the circumstances I could have no objection to his superseding me. A very natural result of my having been ordered to the *Monitor* came to my attention afterwards. There were many officers in the vicinity without commands, who were much senior to me, and who naturally resented a young lieutenant being given such important duty over their heads.

All other survivors of the *Cumberland* and *Congress* had gone on leave, and since no naval substitutes for my zouave uniform could be obtained at Hampton Roads, the loss of my new command was compensated by one month's leave, readily granted.

The new uniforms ordered immediately upon arrival at Boston, were scarcely completed at the end of four days, when telegraphic orders were received to rejoin the fleet at once. Commodore Goldsborough had resumed command at Hampton Roads, and adopted a plan of ramming the *Merrimac* with a number of large fast coastal merchant steamers, chartered for that purpose, should she make another appearance. He acquainted me with this plan, and handed me orders to command the *Illinois,* a steamer of about 3,000 tons, in those days a large vessel.

On my assuming command of the *Illinois* that afternoon, and informing her merchant captain that it was not necessary for him to remain on board longer except on his choice, he protested that no such employment as ramming the formidable *Merrimac* was in the terms of the charter, and at once went ashore to telegraph the owners these intentions. The latter took the matter up in Washington and succeeded in having the charter revoked. Consequently a few days later I lost my new command.

Commodore Goldsborough then gave me a staff

appointment as his flag lieutenant. For several weeks my principal duty was, upon the sighting of smoke in the general direction of Norfolk, to proceed with a message on board of each man-of-war present, that the *"Merrimac* was coming out and the Commodore directed that preparations be made to ram her." So many of these alarms proved false that my message became a standing joke in the fleet.

During this period there was a constant stream of higher officials from Washington who came to visit Hampton Roads, and as flag lieutenant it fell to my lot to assist in looking out for them. One of these, Mr. Gideon Welles, Secretary of the Navy, desired to make an inspection of the entire vicinity. For a trip up the James River the Commodore designated the *Dacotah* to accompany the transport which bore the Secretary and his party, and instructed me to precede these vessels in a tug, as an advance guard and pilot. When we had reached a point beyond which there might be rebel batteries, I advised the Secretary that he should anchor and permit me to reconnoiter higher up. This done, the tug proceeded up the river alone, and after a few miles sighted a rebel flag on a high bank, close to which the channel passed. Approaching this locality cautiously, we could finally make out two guns mounted near the flag staff, but the most careful examination with glasses failed to disclose any people. The absence of soldiers persuaded me that the flag might be captured, and several volunteers in a small boat were sent ashore for this purpose. They found the works entirely abandoned, probably on account of the arrival of such a large force of vessels, and the flag was lowered and brought back to the tug. In great glee I returned to the *Dacotah* and presented the prize to the Secretary who was much pleased. Two years later it was still hanging in his office in the Navy Department.

President Lincoln also came to Hampton Roads during this period. His visit coincided with the operation of the landing of General Wool's forces from Fortress Monroe at Ocean Beach, with the object of taking Norfolk in reverse. It fell to my lot to accompany the President on a tug, while he witnessed this landing and inspected the general vicinity. He was very much preoccupied. He sat out on deck, aloof from everyone else, and appeared extremely tired, careworn, and weighted down with responsibility. Naturally I stood somewhat in awe of him and was reluctant to engage him in conversation, except to answer his enquiries and explain the situation.

General Wool's operations were undertaken because of the report, subsequently confirmed, that the rebels were evacuating Norfolk, in order to reinforce Lee's troops on the Peninsula, which were then hard-pressed by McClellan in his Peninsula campaign. With Norfolk thus weakened and threatened, the situation of the *Merrimac* became precarious, and the rebels wished to take her up the James River; but her draft would not permit passage above a point likely to be uncovered by McClellan's army. These considerations persuaded the rebels to blow her up off Craney Island.

On receipt of reports of her destruction, Commodore Goldsborough sent me in a tug to make a reconnaissance. The *Merrimac* was found to be completely destroyed and we were able to pass Craney Island without opposition and proceed up to Norfolk itself. In his official report of this reconnaissance, Commodore Goldsborough was kind enough to say that it was well done and at considerable danger.

When, on my return, the Commodore was acquainted with the situation about Norfolk, he at once ordered the entire fleet to proceed up the river, with my tug in advance to pilot them in. At a point below the naval hospital, the rebels had constructed a barrier of piling, leaving only a narrow opening for the passage of ships; and here they had anchored the old frigate *United States,* apparently with the intention of sinking her to close the barrier should need arise. The haste with which they had evacuated the place seems to have prevented carrying out such plan. One of our ships, whose name I will not mention, rather stupidly ran on the barrier, and her captain ordered me to take a line to assist in towing her off. Anticipating little success until high water, and having no relish for remaining there several hours, I was guilty of a very poor piece of seamanship. After making fast the line and leaving a good deal of slack, I ordered the tug captain to go ahead full speed. The line parted, and having taken a good strategic position forward of the pilot house, it was difficult for me to hear the loud orders from the ship to return again for another line. Instead, full speed was continued back to the flagship, where, reporting to the Commodore what had happened, I was very glad to have him concur in the suggestion that he needed my services on board.

During the next month, I was engaged in the monotonous though strenuous duty of destroying the great number of batteries which the Confederates had mounted in the river approaches to Norfolk. Experience proved that the method of placing two guns muzzle to muzzle, and destroying one with a shot from the other, was quicker and more certain than attempting to blow up guns individually, by putting in an over charge of powder.

The destruction of batteries completed, I became eager for the command of an active vessel, and obtaining leave of absence, presented my case in person to Mr. Fox, Assistant Secretary, at his office in Washington. He was very kind, but no vessel appropriate to my rank which would fill the requirements, was available. Finally he offered me the command of the *Alligator,* then lying at Washington Navy Yard.

CHAPTER VIII

AT this period there were reports of the construction at Richmond of a new and improved *Merrimac,* called the *Virginia II,* whose possible prowess caused no little anxiety, and moved the Department to consider attacking her with the *Alligator,* a submarine which had been invented by a Frenchman and offered to our Government. Since the boat was very small and the design called for propulsion by man-power, it was anticipated that the principal difficulty would be a supply of fresh air, notwithstanding the inventor's claim of having developed a secret effective chemical means for its purification. A very crude mechanism was providing for attaching a mine to an enemy vessel, after having reached a position under her bottom.

On tendering me the command of this novel craft Secretary Fox said: "Mr. Selfridge, if you will take the *Alligator* up the James River and destroy the *Virginia II,* I will make you a captain." But the probability of the *Alligator's* successful development as a submarine, and of her accomplishing such a difficult task, was against my better judgment, and after explaining the reasons, I declined the offer; renewing my request for the command of a ship holding out a better prospect for effective work. None such being available, at my request I was granted leave and visited my mother in Vermont.

After thinking the matter over for a few days, however, I became conscience-stricken over a possible lack of patriotism, and telegraphed my acceptance to Mr. Fox, who replied with telegraphic directions to report in Washington.

My preliminary inspection of the *Alligator,* then lying at the Washington Navy Yard, was disappointing. She was little more than a cigar-shaped hull with crude man-power propulsion machinery inside. The Frenchman had disappeared, leaving no information as to his secret process of air purification. However, I determined to do my best, and by permission of the Department, went to New York to get a volunteer crew. There, the captain of the receiving ship called the crew to quarters, explained the mission and asked for volunteers. About half of the whole ship's company responded, so that there was little difficulty in picking out fourteen promising looking men to take back to Washington.

The first experiment was made by putting all the crew and myself inside the *Alligator,* closing the manhole, and sinking the vessel by the admission of water, as provided in her design. We remained on the bottom about five minutes and successfully came to the surface again by pumping out the water; the precaution of attaching lines, with which, on signal, she could be raised in the event of difficulty, proving superfluous.

The next venture was to make a short cruise down the river. I remained on deck to con the boat while below the crew worked the crankshafts, each of which was attached to an external paddle, feathered during the forward stroke by closing like a book. Since the feathering 'was only partial, however, much power was lost and great exertions were required to make even a very low speed.

The *Alligator* had proceeded but a short distance on this first cruise, when her bow began to sink rather suddenly, notwithstanding a forward water-tight air compartment. A glance down the man-hole disclosed a rush being made by the men to get out, and then the seriousness of a lack of air supply became strikingly evident. They were hastily cautioned to be careful, to come up one at a time, or the transfer of their weight to the forward end of the ship would sink her. In this way the danger was averted and all the men were finally rescued, though a few were too much exhausted to gain the deck without assistance.

As we drifted helpless down the river, a nearby schooner was hailed, a small boat borrowed from her, and the new-fangled submarine towed back above water to the Navy Yard by the old fashioned propulsion of oars.

This ended my career on the *Alligator*. It was sufficiently demonstrated that she was of no value. Some time later she was lost off Hatteras, while being towed to Charleston, with the intention of using her in an attack on vessels in that harbor.

It was at about this time, in July, 1862, that I passed my examination for the grade of Lieutenant-Commander and was duly promoted thereto.

The failure of the *Alligator* left me still without a command, and in spite of frequent inquiries at the Department, my junior rank denied me any favorable prospects until Commander F. K. Murray (detail officer) suggested that I apply for duty in the Mississippi Squadron. This opportunity was seized gladly, and soon the fourteen volunteers and myself were on our way to Cairo, Illinois, where in August, 1862, we duly reported to Captain Pennock, the Senior Officer at the Naval Base. I was delighted when he issued orders for me to command the ironclad *Cairo* to relieve Commander Nathaniel C. Bryant whose health had failed him, and the *Alligator's* personnel were soon on board a naval transport, bound for Memphis where the *Cairo* was lying.

CHAPTER IX

THE *Cairo* was a fine command. She was 175 feet long by 51½ feet beam, 6 feet draft, and of 600 tons displacement. From one foot above the waterline the sides were inclined at an angle of 35°, and the bow and stern at 45°. Iron plating covered the sloping bow and the sides abreast of the boilers, as well as the conical pilot house forward and the paddle wheel at the stern. Four 32-pounders were carried on each side, three 7-inch guns in the bow ports, and two lighter guns in the stern. The crew comprised about two hundred men.

There were seven gunboats of this type on the Mississippi River; all built at St. Louis on the initiative of Quartermaster-General Meigs of the Army, under contract with the eminent civil engineer James B. Eads, who was assisted by Flag Officer A. H. Foote and Commodore John Rodgers. While the test of service brought out some important defects in these vessels, particularly an insufficiency of armor and a weakness of boiler design, nevertheless on the whole their general performance was quite remarkable. They stood up well under a lot of punishment, incident to extremely active operations which proved their great utility.

My first three months on board the *Cairo* were spent in strengthening her protection, by laying steel rails along the sides to close the gaps between her bow armor and the armor abreast the boilers. Advantage was also taken of the opportunity to improve the fighting qualities of the personnel by constant drills. The officers and crews of these vessels were recruited principally from Mississippi River steamboats, and while inherently excellent men, initially they lacked that degree of military efficiency to be attained only through intensive discipline and training.

At the time I joined the squadron, New Orleans, Memphis, and other main points on the river had all fallen, with the exception of Vicksburg and Port Hudson, which constituted the only important barriers to the free passage of Federal vessels. But in spite of the general control which had been established, the shores between the Federal centers were infested with guerillas, who frequently without warning would open fire on shipping, using rifles or light mobile artillery. These conditions rendered it at all times hazardous, and occasionally difficult, for the gunboats to maintain safe passage for the numerous transports, which served as the principal line of communications for our armies operating in that general vicinity.

In October, 1862, Rear Admiral Porter took command of the naval forces on the Mississippi, which were then for the first time regularly organized into a squadron exclusively under naval control. The Admiral had instructions to co-operate closely with the Army, and history furnishes few examples of this being done more efficiently in the joint operations of land and naval forces.

Soon after Porter's arrival at Cairo, Illinois, General Grant came for a conference and proposed an expedition against Vicksburg. His plan was to march with 60,000 men from Holly Springs upon Grenada, in north central Mississippi, in the hope of inducing the Confederate General Pemberton to leave the intrenchments of Vicksburg, and interpose a superior force against Grant's progress. Meantime Sherman, with 30,000 soldiers, was to proceed on transports under the protection of Porter's gunboats, and land at a point just north of Vicksburg, between that city and the rear of Pemberton. It was hoped that this would give Sherman an opportunity to capture the great Confederate stronghold before Pemberton could return.

The point selected for Sherman's debarkation was about twenty miles up the Yazoo River, and preliminary to the landing it was necessary to reconnoiter that river, and clear it of numerous torpedoes known to have been placed there by the Confederates. Accordingly, on December 11th the first reconnaissance was made by two "tin-clads" —ordinary river steamers converted to naval use and lightly armored. But their efforts were frustrated by the enemy's light artillery, and numerous sharpshooters in rifle pits which lined the left bank of the Yazoo.

The manifest importance of clearing out the torpedoes before Sherman's arrival, moved me to volunteer to take the *Cairo* and another iron-clad up the river, in support of the "tin-clads." We were greeted by showers of bullets from the rifle pits and frequent fire from the batteries, but by the two gunboats enfilading those positions while the "tin-clads" dragged for the torpedoes, we were able to make fair progress. On December 12th, however, the *Cairo* got into serious difficulties. The "tin-clad," *Marmora,* in advance, encountered unusually strong resistance, and appeared to be sorely beset by the enemy sharpshooters. The *Cairo* hastened ahead to give support, when she struck a floating torpedo. Two explosions occurred in quick succession, which seemed to lift the vessel out of the water, and notwithstanding every effort to keep her afloat, she sank in twelve minutes, leaving nothing but the tops of her chimneys showing above six fathoms of water. All hands were saved.

In his *Naval History of the Civil War,* Admiral Porter said:

"No fault was imputed to the commanding officer of the *Cairo*. It was an accident liable to occur to any gallant officer whose zeal carries him to the post of danger and who is loath to let others do what he thinks he ought to do himself.". . . . "The Admiral looked upon it simply as an accident of war, and Selfridge was immediately given command of the *Conestoga.*"

After the loss of the *Cairo* her entire complement took passage on a transport for Cairo, Illinois. On the way we fell in with Admiral Porter in his flagship the *Black Hawk,* and I repaired on board and reported the circumstances of the *Cairo's* end. He was very sympathetic and kind, and gave me immediate orders to the *Conestoga;* a river steamer which had been converted to naval use, but much to my regret, was not suitable for participating in the subsequent operations of the squadron on the Yazoo River with Sherman.

For several months the *Conestoga* was engaged in patrolling the Mississippi to guard the Army's line of supply. From her principal station off the mouth of the White River, she was required to insure the safe passage of supply steamers and transports between that point and the mouth of the Arkansas River, a distance of about twenty-five miles. We had frequent skirmishes with the guerillas and their mobile shore batteries of 6-pounders' but our 32-pounders were always able to put them to rout. Whenever the rebels seemed to be operating from a plantation, we would land and set fire to the buildings. We also made a number of reconnaissances, either with the ship or her boats, up the White River and Arkansas River, and occasionally we landed in an effort to capture guerilla forces, but rarely were we successful in this.

Since there were rebel vessels up both the White River and the Arkansas River, and since the *Conestoga* could not be in two places at the same time, I was never quite sure when damage might be done to the frequent transports passing in both directions, by a raid out of one or the other of these rivers. A sketch of this locality is shown to illustrate this difficulty more clearly.

The guerillas were particularly active on a long, narrow point which projected into the river just north of Island No. 74. One morning it was noticed that the high river had partially flooded the narrow neck connecting the long point with the mainland, and it occurred to me that if even a small flow of water could be started across this neck, a deep channel would soon be eroded by the river itself; thus affording a short cut between the limiting points of my station. A boat's crew made short work of digging the necessary few hundred yards of ditch, and before many hours a raging torrent was rapidly enlarging the cut, carrying away even large trees. The next morning, from our anchorage north of the neck, a number of transports were sighted standing down river, and in accordance with the usual custom we spoke them and reported "All clear," whereupon they proceeded around the great bend of about eighteen miles. I said to myself "Now is the time to try the cut-off," and decided to take the *Conestoga* through it to the mouth of the Arkansas River, and thus afford the maximum protection to the transports. It was a decision involving danger, which only youth would justify.

In the first place, the current in the new cut must have approached 12 knots in strength, so that once entered, the ship would no longer be under control and nothing but luck could govern the subsequent rapid drift. Secondly, there was no means of estimating the depth of water in the new channel, nor of knowing that it was clear of dangerous snags from the numerous trees which had been washed into it. However, these considerations failed to dampen a youthful ardor, and after standing up river for a good start, we headed for the cut at full speed so as to maintain steerage-way as long as possible. Luck served me well. We shot through without serious difficulty, and then waited off the mouth of the Arkansas River for the transports to appear. As the latter approached we could sense their utter amazement at seeing the *Conestoga* there, after having spoken and passed her eighteen miles back on their course. The captain of the leading transport hailed me and said,

"What in hell are you doing here?" to which I replied, "Why, I came through the cut-off. Didn't you see me?" He said "No,—what cut-off?" and then the mystery was explained to him.

A peculiar sequel to this experiment was the destruction of the town of Napoleon, in former days one of a number of notorious river gambling headquarters. The Selfridge cut-off so changed the course of the river as to wash away the whole townsite, and the property owners very seriously considered suing me for damages.

In the main the patrol duty was monotonous, and to me rather irksome, particularly since I felt that the unfortunate loss of the *Cairo* had kept me from participating in the active and interesting work of assisting Sherman's first and unsuccessful attempt before Vicksburg, and his subsequent attack upon Fort Hindman, up the Arkansas River. In the latter, the operations of the gunboats proved especially valuable and conspicuous, but for such work the *Conestoga* was unsuited, owing to the lack of any armor.

Naturally, a part of my duties was to keep informed of rebel shore activities along my section of the river, which could be done very well through negroes, many of whom were anxious to help the "Yankees." One afternoon a Confederate officer was reported to have arrived at a nearby house, after swimming his horse across the Mississippi. Landing that night with a few men, we surrounded the house, and captured both officer and horse. I may as well confess to a greater interest in the capture of the latter than the former, since only a very fine animal could swim the great river. Both prizes were shipped to Cairo by the next northbound transport, together with a note to Captain Pennock, which resulted in the horse being bid in for me at the auction sale prescribed for all captured property. Several months afterwards the horse nearly cost me my life. I had had him shipped to Boston, and frequently used to drive him while there on leave. One day he was frightened by a locomotive whistle, and ran away, along that part of Beacon Street then being projected by a fill, abreast the Public Gardens. The buggy barely escaped being wrecked at high speed, against a large truck.

While in the foregoing case, information from the negroes led me into peril, in another it saved me from Libby Prison, and made me eternally grateful to their race. About ten miles inland from Skipwith Landing, where the *Conestoga* habitually went for coal, there lived a widow named Mrs. Walton. My acquaintance with her originated through a letter from Captain Pennock (at Cairo), asking me to give her safe conduct on the occasion of her return via transport to her plantation, from a visit to New York. During the *Conestoga's* coaling periods I frequently rode to her house, and lunched there. On Christmas morning, 1862, when about half way to the plantation, a negro emerged from the roadside brush ahead and held up his hand. Reining in my horse I enquired, "What do you want, Uncle?" He replied, "Massa, I think you had better not go to Mrs. Walton's today." Further questions brought out the fact that a trap to capture me had been laid by a party of about fifty Confederate soldiers, who had learned of my frequent visits. Their plan had been discovered by the negroes, who promptly sent the messenger to warn me. Since all Yankees captured at that time were sent to Libby Prison, I consider my escape to have been especially fortunate, and have always felt most grateful to the negroes for it.

In the course of time the *Conestoga's* boilers became in urgent need of repairs, and on my recommendation she was sent to Cairo, Illinois, for that purpose; her personnel, however, being transferred to the *Manitou,* a side-wheeler gunboat converted from a river steamer. The *Manitou* lacked sufficient armor protection to place her in the same class with the iron-clads built by Mr. Eads, but she had a heavy battery of two 8-inch guns forward. By this time the complicated maneuvers of our armies around Vicksburg, which I need not describe, had resulted in that city being invested by the combined armies of Grant and Sherman.

Sherman on the north flank, being embarrassed by a certain Confederate battery, requested Admiral Porter to land some naval artillery. The

Manitou's 8-inch guns were selected for that purpose, and transferred to emplacements which had been constructed by Sherman's soldiers, on the edge of a ravine lying between the two lines.

In his *Naval History of the Civil War*, Admiral Porter said:

"Lieutenant Commander Selfridge had command of the naval battery on the right wing in General Sherman's Corps. This battery was worked with marked ability and elicited the warmest praise from the Commanding General. One thousand shells were fired from Lieutenant Commander Selfridge's guns. His services being required up the river, I relieved him a few days before the surrender."

The experience ashore with Sherman had many interesting aspects. While the rebel artillery opposite to us was soon silenced, we were constantly harassed by rifle fire from sharpshooters, who crept into the ravine in advance of their line. To protect ourselves against this, we built a curtain consisting of a large hawser flaked down and sewed together, secured between two layers of stout board. This was raised to cover the gun port whenever the gun was run in on its naval carriage for loading.

The sailor-like arrangements made in our camp excited much curiosity among the soldiers. We constructed a single large tent for the guns' crews, and made it as shipshape as possible. All men slept in hammocks, and we had nautical mess tables and mess gear, and a flooring not dissimilar to a ship's deck. These features so interested and amused the army that a constant swarm of soldiers frequented our camp, especially upon the weekly occasions when the tent "deck" was taken outside in sections, and "holy-stoned" in true sailor fashion. We never failed to have a large audience on these "field-days."

General Sherman was very kind to me. He furnished me with a horse, and almost daily we would ride together down the lines, usually going as far as General Grant's headquarters in the center. Sherman was a very sociable and attractive companion, and I became very fond of him.

After a few weeks of this interesting service, it became manifest that Vicksburg must soon fall; preparations were made to send naval expeditions up the Yazoo and Red Rivers to clear those vicinities of rebels, and when the *Conestoga* returned from Cairo after the completion of her repairs, Admiral Porter ordered me back to her. Lieutenant Commander John G. Walker relieved me from charge of the shore battery, only four days before Vicksburg surrendered.

CHAPTER X

Soon after the fall of Vicksburg on July 4, 1863, I received orders from Admiral Porter to conduct a raid up the Red River, with the *Conestoga* as flagship, and the gunboats *Manitou, Rattler, Forest Rose, Petrel,* and *Curlew.* The general purpose of the expedition was to make such captures of cotton and other stores as might prove practicable, and to drive Confederate forces away from the vicinity of the mouth of the Red River, and from two of its tributaries, the Black and Tensas Rivers. At the head of navigation of the latter stream, which ran approximately parallel to the Mississippi, there was an extensive area of navigable waters called Tensas Lake and Bayou Macon, which reached to within five or six miles of the Mississippi River. From the intervening narrow strip of land, parties of enemy riflemen were in the habit of firing upon transports traversing the Mississippi, sometimes injuring women and children on board.

The large force of Confederates in this region believed themselves safe from attack by gunboats, owing to the difficulties of the water approaches to the Tensas Lake and the Bayou Macon. However, we proceeded up the Red River, and then up the Black and Tensas Rivers, both narrow streams, and on July 12th surprised the rebels by appearing on the Lake and the Bayou. We caught sight of a number of transports, but they succeeded in escaping among the maze of uncharted channels, where we could not follow promptly without pilots, and reached the protection of the fort at Harrisonburg. Receiving information of a large quantity of ammunition that had just been hauled from Natchez, a landing party succeeded in capturing it.

That night was very dark and rainy, but before daylight the next morning, the gunboats were divided and started on a search of various channels. The *Manitou* and *Rattler* were sent up the Little Red River (a small tributary of the Black River), while the *Forest Rose* and *Petrel* explored the Tensas. The former detachment discovered and took possession of the *Louisville,* one of the largest and best river steamers remaining in the possession of the Confederates. She was subsequently converted into a United States man-of-war, carrying 40 brass howitzers. The *Forest Rose* and *Petrel* captured a steamer called the *Elmira,* having a cargo of stores, sugar, and rum, for the Confederate Army. In the afternoon I went on board the *Rattler* and reconnoitered the mouth of the Tensas

River. We passed great quantities of cotton which had been set on fire, and sighted a body of Rebel cavalry, which a few rounds of shrapnel persuaded to retreat to a safe distance, but saw no shipping.

On the 14th, leaving the *Petrel* in charge of the prizes, the remainder of the squadron started up the Ouachita River for a further reconnaissance towards Fort Harrisonburg. We anchored that night some distance below the fort, keeping the crews at their guns. At 5 a.m. the *Conestoga* and *Manitou* got under way and stood up to within two miles of the fort, which did not reply to a few shells from our battery. A thick fog coming on, at about 6 a.m. the gunboats were withdrawn down the river. The reconnaissance disclosed nothing afloat below the fort, which contained guns too heavy to be trifled with by wooden gunboats.

Admiral Porter was much pleased with the success of the expedition. Besides the capture of the *Louisville* and *Elmira,* we had caused the rebels to burn two other small steamers, to prevent their falling into our hands, and had taken such a considerable quantity of stores and ammunition, as must have seriously embarrassed the further operations of the Confederate Army under General Walker. These munitions included 15,000 rounds of smooth-bore ammunition, 1,000 rounds of Enfield ammunition, 20 rounds of 12-pounder shell, 154 rounds of 6-pounder ammunition and 50 Parrott shell.

After this raid the *Conestoga* spent several months guarding the Mississippi River, in the vicinity of the mouth of the Red River, during which there occurred two incidents that seem worth mentioning. One afternoon while anchored in mid-river, rifle fire was opened on the ship by a company of Confederates, who had gained the shelter of the western levee, apparently safe from our guns. The ship got under way quickly and moved near the eastern shore, out of rifle range, but since they persisted in annoying us with their fire, I determined to try a system of mortar fire with our main battery. These guns were set at high elevation and fired with a reduced charge, in the hope that the angle of fall would be so great as possibly to hit close inside the levee. The first shot falling short, a larger charge was tried and resulted in an "over." The next charge, and hence the range, was reduced slightly. In this way, by trial and error, after a few shots, we managed to land two shells in their midst, apparently wounding some of them, and they retreated in short order. Probably this is one of very few occasions when naval guns have been used as mortars.

The second incident of note occurred on February 13, 1864. Learning through negroes of a quantity of Confederate Government cotton being under a small guard of soldiers, about five miles inland, the writer landed in the early morning with forty-five seamen and about an equal number of negroes.[1] A short distance from the landing place we unexpectedly came upon two Confederate officers, engaged in getting breakfast at what had apparently been their camp for the previous night, who were so taken by surprise that they could do nothing but surrender. They proved to be Colonel Charles H. Tyler and Major John F. O'Brien, both West Point graduates and officers of our regular army before the war, and were sent back to the ship as prisoners of war. Continuing the search for the cotton, we came upon it about six miles from the landing point, loaded in wagons from which the mules had been unhitched. Except for the accidental discharge of a musket we would have captured the guard at breakfast, but they made good their escape.

So far the expedition had been eminently successful, but the most difficult part was still before us. About 2,500 Confederate soldiers under General Polignac were known to be in the general vicinity, and there was every reason to assume that information from the escaping guard would soon menace our difficult retreat with the slow moving, heavily laden wagon. The perversity of mule nature cost an anxious and valuable hour of delay. They did not like stranger masters, and objected to

[1] Owing to the shortage in the crew, negroes had been employed as a regular part of the ship's company for fireroom duty, and did good service in that capacity. Many of them became good shots with the rifle, which explains their participation in the landing force on this occasion.

doing duty in any but their accustomed places
which were unknown to us, so that many redistri-
butions of balky mules were necessary before a fair
start could be made.

This triumph was scarcely accomplished before
a party of rebel cavalrymen appeared and began
charging us with a yell. Hastily seeking the protection of the cotton wagons, we checked the charge
by several volleys and proceeded on our way.
Shortly afterwards another charge was begun, and
stopped by the same tactics, but it was evident that
the expected arrival of large enemy reinforcements
would end in our defeat. In this extremity a
vedette was dispatched in haste back to the ship,
with instructions for her to open fire with the main
battery, in the general direction of the fight. This
expedient served us well in persuading the Confederates to desist in their attacks, and we succeeded in reaching the river, and embarking all of
the cotton, mules, and wagons without the loss of
a single man, although a number of the enemy were
seen to have been hit.

Not long after this incident, Admiral Porter and
General Banks reached an agreement to undertake
a joint expedition up the Red River to Shreveport,
and the *Conestoga* was sent to Vicksburg to bring
down ammunition for the fleet. On the return
trip the ship was run into and sunk, during the
night of March 8th, by the steamer *General Price*.
The writer had turned in several hours before this

collision, leaving a pilot in charge on deck, and was awakened by one blast from our whistle, followed almost immediately by two blasts from another whistle. The "crossed whistles" were sufficient warning of danger, and jumping out of bed I rushed to the bridge just as the two ships collided. The good old *Conestoga* went down in about four minutes, but due to the prompt action of Acting Volunteer Lieutenant J. F. Richardson, commanding the *General Price,* in lowering her boats, all hands were saved except two seamen.

Thus for the third time in the war, I had had my ship suddenly sunk under me. It is a strange coincidence that the names of these three ships all begin with the letter "C," and that two of these disasters occurred on the 8th day of March; the other on the 12th of December.

The responsibility for this accident clearly rested on the officer of the deck of the *General Price,* in the absence of her captain who was asleep below. It is a rule of the road on the Mississippi, that a vessel standing down river has the right of way, since she is less easily controlled than one proceeding against the current. Moreover the *Conestoga's* single whistle blast indicated her intention to pass in the natural way, by each of the two steamers merely continuing on her course, leaving the other to port. An answer of one blast from the *General Price* would have established mutual understanding on this, the normal basis. But her two blasts introduced confusion, by declaring a purpose of crossing our bow and passing on the opposite or starboard side, which regardless of the question of right of way, was poor seamanship.

The *General Price* took the survivors back to the fleet, and on my reporting to Admiral Porter he remarked, "Well, Selfridge, you do not seem to have much luck with the top of the alphabet. I think that for your next ship I will try the bottom." I was given command of the iron-clad *Osage,* and on the opportunity presenting itself many months later, the Admiral went still farther down the alphabet to the *Vindicator!* But the story of the *Osage* comes first.

CHAPTER XI

The *Osage,* to which I was assigned just previous to the Red River Expedition, was a stern-wheeled iron-clad, drawing about five feet of water, and carrying a battery of two 11-inch guns, mounted forward in a turret protected by six inches of armor. Although inferior to the *Cairo* type, still she was a good ship with a fine crew, which was augmented by the fourteen volunteers who had been kept with me since the days of the *Alligator.*

I wish especially to mention the Chief Engineer, William Doughty, who had originally come from the Mississippi River steamboat service, and was a man of much intelligence and resource. For example, on my arrival he called attention to a serious deficiency of fighting power, in that the turret could not be trained more than a few degrees either side of dead ahead, owing to damaged teeth in some of the gearing. The turret was very heavy, weighing nearly seventy-two tons; nevertheless he suggested that by jacking it up, the defective pinion could be turned into a new position and the angle of train thus greatly increased. After borrowing all the jacks in the fleet and working very hard for several days, Mr. Doughty succeeded in making a good job of these repairs. As will appear later this served us in good stead under critical circumstances.

Doughty also suggested a method of sighting the turret from the outside, by means of what would now be called a periscope, although at that time such a device had never been heard of. Encouraged to proceed with the development of his novel idea, he mounted two sights on top of the turret, and paralleled them with the axes of the guns in the vertical plane. Immediately behind the rear sight was placed a mirror, turned downwards 45°, and mounted in the upper end of a tube, extending down several feet outside and in the rear of the turret. At the lower end of this tube was another mirror, parallel to the first. By this arrangement, a person standing behind the turret and looking into the lower mirror, would see reflected the two sights, as well as distant objects in the same line. I did not expect the contrivance to be of great use but developed it more as an interesting experiment, but as will be described later, it proved of extraordinary utility.

On March 11th, General A. J. Smith from Sherman's army, joined the assembled fleet with 10,000 soldiers in transports, in accordance with a plan by which General Banks was to be reinforced for the land expedition up the Red River. Banks had informed Admiral Porter that he would march with 36,000 men to Alexandria, Louisiana, and desired to meet Porter and Smith there on the 17th of March. To make this junction, the fleet together with Smith's transports started up the Red River on the 12th, with the preliminary intention of taking Fort De Russy, which constituted the main defence of the lower Red River.

About two miles below the fort was encountered a formidable obstruction to navigation. Two lines of heavy piling well braced together, extended completely across the river, and were protected on the down-stream side by a raft of heavy timber, partly on the bottom. The whole was covered by entangled branches of large trees, which had been floated down upon the piling, and the river was apparently impassable. In order to avoid unnecessary delay General Smith's troops were landed under the protection of nine gunboats, while the remaining four, the *Eastport, Osage, Fort Hindman,* and *Cricket,* were put to work to clear a passage through the obstruction. This proved much easier than seemed possible in the beginning. The piles near the banks were first removed, and the rush of water through the small openings assisted the work of pulling up and removing the remaining piles. Twelve hours of strenuous labor resulted in gaining sufficient width to permit passage of the fleet; then the four gunboats which had breeched the obstruction proceeded off Fort De Russy where the advance of General Smith had arrived.

Fort De Russy was a formidable work, probably one of the strongest constructed by the Confederates during the war. Besides the protection given by earthworks, exposed positions had been armored with railroad iron. The garrison comprised 5,000 men under General Walker, who marched out to meet Smith's army with all but 300 of them. Walker was defeated in the open, and Smith then took the Fort by assault, without much difficulty. In these operations the gunboat could be of little use, because the nature of the country made it difficult to observe the progress of the land operations, and there was great danger of firing into our own forces.

The fleet, with A. J. Smith's transports and army, then proceeded up river to Alexandria, which was reached two days ahead of the scheduled time, but General Banks failed to appear until ten days afterwards. Meantime, the river level being too low for the fleet to pass over the falls just above Alexandria, Admiral Porter directed me to "pick up some cotton" while he awaited the arrival of Banks. Accordingly I assumed temporary command of one of the smaller gunboats, and went back down the river with an empty transport, in search of cotton.

It should be explained here that the Navy's frequent captures of cotton were in accord with a general policy of the Federal Government, that cotton was contraband of war and should be seized wherever found, unless Union ownership could be established. It was one of those measures adopted to bring pressure upon the morale of the civilian population of the Confederacy, and as such it doubtless proved very effective, since war conditions had advanced the price of cotton to about $400 a bale when landed at a seaport. Of course, captured cotton was duly sent in for adjudication before a prize court, and the proceeds went to the Federal treasury, except that portion prescribed by law for distribution as prize money to the captors. The incentive of prize money naturally influenced the Navy to be especially active in this work. On the other hand, the high price led to a great deal of dishonesty among the owners, and the cotton speculators who made a business of buying from them. In nearly every case of captured cotton, the owner would endeavor to prove to the prize court that he was really a Union man; whereas as a matter of fact, especially in the Red River country, genuine sympathy and loyalty to the Union cause was almost non-existent. The legal difficulties of establishing the non-Union ownership of captured cotton, led my crew to resort to an expedient which, while not entirely ethical, may have been justified by the special conditions. They made stencils of the letters "C.S.A." (Confederate States of America) and would so mark captured cotton. While I did not authorize this procedure, I knew of and winked at it.

The raid with the gunboat and transport resulted in the capture of 700 or 800 bales in all. One incident seems worthy of mention. A landing party had just finished seizing the cotton from a plantation belonging to a Brigadier in the Confederate Army, when they moved to the next plantation and also seized the cotton there. The owner of the latter was really a Union man though so old that the Confederates had not molested him. While his property was on its way to the ship, he appeared on board, greatly excited, and exhibited convincing documentary proof of his Union sentiments and affiliations. He then very feelingly protested somewhat as follows:

"Captain, a strange thing has occurred which I can account for in no other way, except that some enemies of mine have tried to injure me. I find that my cotton has been marked 'C.S.A.' without my knowledge. It does not belong to the Confederate Government, but to myself and I have had no dealings with that Government."

With difficulty restraining my amusement at the situation, I assured him that his papers were sufficient proof of his loyalty, and without further explanation directed that his goods be hauled back to the plantation. During this raid, the Confederates set fire to large quantities of cotton, to prevent its falling into our hands, thus producing a haze over the entire vicinity, so thick as to resemble a fog.

I reached Alexandria and resumed command of the *Osage,* several days before General Banks' arrival on the 25th of March. Meantime advantage had been taken of a rise in the river, to pass the gunboats over the falls, together with the twenty transports which had brought General Smith's army.

On March 31st, the advance guard of the fleet, comprising eight gunboats including the *Osage,* proceeded up river without special incident to Grand Ecore, to be ready to cover the army when it reached that point after a march overland. Our greatest difficulty was an insufficient supply of coal, which made it necessary to rely upon wood from shore. Each night the transports and gunboats would tie up to the bank, send ashore landing parties preceded by pickets, and gather fence rails for the next day's supply of fuel. If the rebels had been clever enough to burn rails, instead of cotton, the naval participation in the expedition would have been greatly hindered above Alexandria.

On April 2d, General Kilby Smith embarked his command on transports, and proceeded under convoy of the remainder of the fleet to Grand Ecore, where it was again landed. From this point

Banks' whole army began an advance on April 6th, arranging to meet the fleet three days later at Springfield Landing, where we arrived on the appointed day. The army, however, did not put in an appearance, and the Admiral soon learned that it had been defeated by the Confederates. I was apprised of this situation when Porter sent for me, and explained that Banks' defeat, leaving a victorious rebel army between him and the fleet, made it necessary for us to fall back. He instructed me to bring up the rear in the *Osage,* as a guard to the transports, which were to follow the main force of gunboats.

CHAPTER XII

VERY soon after starting down river from Springfield Landing, there occurred an episode of considerable importance, which I described to Admiral Porter, at his request, in a letter of June 2, 1880, quoted below.

"NEWPORT, R. I., June 2d, 1880.

"ADMIRAL D. D. PORTER, Washington, D.C.

"Dear Sir: Fifteen years have elapsed since the fatal repulse of a portion of the rebel trans-Mississippi forces under their General Green, by the gunboats *Osage* and *Lexington* of your fleet, and for the first time I have learned of the report of General Kilby Smith, before the "Committee upon the Conduct of the War," in which he claims for the transports under his command the principal merit of the victory.

"The fight took place at what was known as Blair's plantation, and in saying it was essentially a gunboat fight, no reflection is cast upon the portion of A. J. Smith's division embarked on the transports, because it was never designed they should engage a powerful force from their steamers; nor were the latter capable of a prolonged engagement, such as actually took place, from the unprotected condition of their hulls.

"The facts of the fight are briefly these: On the afternoon of April 11th, we first learned of the repulse of Banks' army at Sabine Cross Roads, which forced the return of the transports and of the fleet under your command. You directed me (at that time in command of the light-draft Monitor *Osage*) to bring up and protect the rear.

"The river was very low, and the swift current in the bends made the *Osage* almost unmanageable while descending. For this reason, the next morning, April 12th, I lashed the transport *Black Hawk* on my starboard quarter, and by her assistance made the descent successfully, till late in the afternoon, when we grounded on the point opposite Blair's plantation. Our bow was therefore pointed down stream, and our starboard broadside opposite the right bank, which was 20 feet high and 100 yards distant. The transports had necessarily passed down, as my position was in the rear. Seeing my situation, Bache, of the *Lexington,* which had stopped near by, came on board. We had been for some time vainly trying to get the *Osage* afloat when the pilot of the *Black Hawk,* who, from his elevated position, could see over the bank, reported a large force issuing from the woods, some two miles back. I ascended to the pilot-house, and from their being dressed in Federal overcoats thought they were our troops; but soon their movements—dismounting and picketing their horses—convinced me they were enemies. I accordingly descended, made all preparations for battle, and directed Bache to go below with the *Lexington,* and take up an enfilading position.

"Then commenced one of the most curious fights of the war, 2,500 infantry against a gunboat aground. The battery unlimbered some hundred yards below and abreast of the *Lexington,* which opened upon it with her port broadside, while I sent a few raking shells from the *Osage* in the same direction. Compelled to plant their guns close to the edge of the bank in order to reach us, on account of the low stage of the river, they could not long maintain the situation, and soon retired with the loss of one gun dismounted.

"By this time my attention was wholly directed to the attack upon my own vessel. The rebels came rapidly across the fields in column of regiments, so the pilot of the *Black Hawk* reported, who alone from his elevated position, could see beyond the bank. So rapid was the advance that this pilot, intent on watching them, stayed too long, and dared not leave the protection of the iron shield of the pilot-house, and so accurate was the fire, that after the fight no fewer than 60 bullet marks were counted upon the shield, behind which the poor fellow was hiding.

"I loaded our two 11-inch guns with canister, elevated just to clear the top of the right bank, and as the heads of the first line became visible, fired.

"One regiment would come up, deliver its fire, then fall back under cover, and another advance. It was necessary carefully to reserve our fire until the rebels were about to fire, or our shots would have gone over them to the rear, a condition of affairs which made gunboat firing very inaccurate at a low stage of water.

"The fire of 2,500 rifles at point-blank range, mingled with the slow, sullen roar of our two great guns, was something indescribable. No transports of wood could have stood such a terrible fire; the few soldiers on the *Black Hawk* sought refuge on the *Osage* while the frightened crew of the steamer stowed themselves in her hold. During the three-quarters of an hour that this singular combat lasted, I had expended every round of grape and canister, and was using shrapnel with fuzes cut to one second, when the firing suddenly ceased and the enemy drew off. During the latter part of the engagement I noticed an officer on a white horse, some 200 yards below the troops, and aiming one of our guns at him, when the smoke cleared away saw him no longer. I learned after that the officer killed was their General Green. The rebel loss was reported at 700, while ours was only seven wounded. The destructiveness of the *Osage's* fire, delivered at point-blank range, was much increased by an ingenious device by which I could personally aim the guns from the outside of the turret, and thus have a clear view of the field, which would have been impossible had I remained inside. The woodwork of the *Black Hawk* and *Osage* was so pitted with bullet holes that it is no exaggeration to say that one could not place the hand anywhere without covering a shot-mark.

"These are the prominent facts. It is very certain no transports were in sight from my decks; they may have been a little below, concealed by the bend, but too far to have had any influence upon the result, the whole brunt of which fell upon the *Osage.* The battery unlimbered abreast of the *Lexington* and was driven off by her fire. No better proof of the absence of General Smith's transports from the fight can be cited than the fact that none of them, except the *Black Hawk,* showed any marks, while she was literally riddled with bullets. There might have been a small gun on the *Black Hawk* but it was never fired. As to the siege-guns on the exposed forecastle of the *Rob Roy,* if fired, it was at too long range to have been of any service.

"The importance of this engagement cannot be over-estimated, for though they had practically possession of both banks of Red River, the rebels hardly molested us during the remainder of our descent as far as Alexandria, excepting the time when they attempted to intercept you by planting batteries against the *Cricket* bearing your flag, and which were so gallantly run by.

"I remain, yours truly,

"THOMAS O. SELFRIDGE,

"Commander, U. S. N."

In the foregoing account mention has been made of the periscope. Its use came about in this way. On first sounding to general quarters, the writer went inside the turret to direct its fire, but the restricted vision from the peep holes rendered it impossible to see what was going on in the threatened quarter, whenever the turret was trained into the loading position. In this extremity I thought of the periscope, and hastily took up station there, well protected by the turret, yet able to survey the whole scene and to direct an accurate fire.

After the rebels had retired, a hasty inspection ashore disclosed a great number of killed and wounded lying about. Several of the poor wounded who had crawled down to the river for water, were taken on board, but the need for haste in getting the ship off the shoal and proceeding with the general retreat, prevented our rendering any further assistance. The rebels subsequently acknowledged a loss of 700 men in this fight, amongst whom was their commander, General

Green, the best partisan General west of the Mississippi. I asked the wounded prisoners why they had been so persistent and headlong in attacking a gunboat, and from them learned that the force was a recently recruited and inexperienced lot of Texans, who had been told by their officers that the gunboats would surrender, if attacked in a determined way.

The remainder of the fleet had delayed its progress, on account of the sound of firing in our direction, but by 10 P.M. the whole force was proceeding towards Pleasant Hill Landing, the next point where a Confederate attack was anticipated. There the Harrison battery attempted to arrest the fleet's progress, as we ran by at daylight the next morning, under cover of a shower of shell, grape, and canister, from the gunboats, which kept down the enemy's fire and prevented them doing us much damage. After passing this battery, little trouble was experienced from the enemy except the constant fire of sharpshooters along the banks. Delay was occasioned, however, by the frequent grounding of transports, owing to a fall in the river since the fleet had passed up. At the village of Campte, much confusion was caused by many vessels grounding. Since this position was only twelve miles above Grand Ecore, where Banks had retreated, Admiral Porter proceeded there in the *Cricket* to request the assistance of the army, and upon landing met General A. J. Smith, who promptly sent a force of about 2,000 men to clear the banks in our vicinity.

The next day, April 15th, all vessels arrived at Grand Ecore safely and in good condition, effecting a junction with the army. The combined forces were quite strong enough to make a fresh advance and to gain Shreveport, the main objective of the expedition, but General Banks decided upon a retreat to Alexandria. The *Lexington* and *Osage* were detailed to convoy the transports in advance of the fleet, and reached the falls at Alexandria without incident. But the remainder of the gunboats were delayed by low water in the Red River, and one of the largest of them, the *Eastport,* was sunk by a torpedo eight miles below Grand Ecore. The Admiral returned in the *Cricket* to render assistance, and succeeded in putting her in condition to proceed; but later she ran hard aground, and on April 26th it was finally necessary to blow her up. On the further retreat, the *Cricket* accompanied by two other gunboats, ran past an ambush of strong Confederate forces of infantry and artillery, and during the four minutes under fire, the *Cricket* was struck thirty-eight times with shell, and many more times with rifle bullets. Twelve men were killed and nineteen wounded. This was one of the closest calls that Porter ever had.

While the army was amply strong, and its communications sufficiently secure, to remain indefinitely at Alexandria, the determination of Banks to retreat still farther rendered the fleet's situation very precarious. The river had fallen until the falls were impassable, and moreover a rise of nearly 14 feet was needed for the fleet's further progress from below the falls to the Mississippi. The sources of the latter river lay among melting snow and ice, accumulated during the Winter, which could be counted on at that season to produce a substantial rise, that would back into the Red River as far as the falls, and thus probably overcome that part of our difficulty. The headwaters of the Red River, however, were much farther south where snow did not fall, and the river level depended upon very irregular rains, so that there seemed little prospect of a sufficient rise above the falls to float the gunboats over them.

From this precarious situation the fleet was saved primarily through the attainments of Colonel Bailey, an engineer officer on General Franklin's staff, who had been in the lumbering business, and was familiar with methods employed to raise river levels for the passage of lumber rafts. Colonel Bailey proposed to deepen the Red River in the same way, and at Admiral Porter's request, he was allowed to proceed with the construction of a special kind of dam just below the falls, assisted by a large number of soldiers and all of the facilities of the fleet.

From each bank a bulkhead was projected toward the middle of the river, until only a gap of about 100 feet remained. On one side of the river the obstruction consisted of a great number of cottonwood saplings, with their butts up stream and weighted with rocks and heavy materials hauled from the vicinity. Each tree had to be placed by the soldiers who worked up to their waists in water. The bulkhead from the other bank was built of wooden cribs, sunk in place by loading them with heavy debris.

The completion of this partial dam, in two sections, resulted in a substantial rise in the river, but still the depth over the falls was insufficent. The gap was then closed further by placing a large coal barge, loaded down with broken machinery, abreast the end of each dam section. Since the current in the gap was exceedingly strong, probably amounting to eight or ten knots an hour, the barges had to be secured by stout hawsers leading to the banks. With this arrangement, enough additional rise was produced to accommodate the lighter draft vessels.

During the latter part of the foregoing operations, Admiral Porter became quite ill and, making me temporary Fleet Captain, left me in charge of transferring the fleet over the falls. The *Lexington* was the first to make the attempt. Just previously the swift current had parted the hawsers securing one of the barges, which was consequently thrown against a prominent rock close below the dam, where it was bilged and sunk. This proved to be an exceedingly fortunate accident. As the *Lexington* approached the gap, the current prevented any further control and she was thrown against the barge, bounced off, and shot safely below without damage. But for the fender action of the barge, she would undoubtedly have been wrecked on the rock, and had she stuck there, would have blocked the further passage of the fleet.

The *Osage* was the next vessel through, followed by the *Neosho* (a sister ship of the *Osage*), both being saved by the wrecked barge from destruction on the rock, just as the *Lexington* had been.

In spite of lightening the larger gunboats, by stripping much of their armor and landing their broadside guns, there was not enough water on the falls for them to pass. Colonel Bailey again came to the rescue with the construction of "wing dams," located several hundred yards above the main dam. These consisted of a series of light dams which constricted the channel abreast the shallowest part, and served to raise the level an additional foot, and thus permit the safe passage of all except the largest of the vessels. She drew about six inches too much water. In this predicament I sought the assistance of a kind friend in the army, a colonel, who offered the services of his regiment with its band. A 4-inch hawser was led from the ship to the shore, and 2,000 men dragged her over the falls, stamping their feet in unison with the inspiring music from the regimental band.

Almost immediately after this the last of the army evacuated Alexandria, notwithstanding that twelve 32-pounders which had been landed to lighten the larger gunboats, still remained on a sand spit above the falls. Not caring to leave these behind, at daybreak the next morning I took several boats to the spit, and began destroying the guns by firing one into another, muzzle to muzzle. While this was in progress we sighted the approach of formidable rebel forces who were not slow in opening fire, but just as the last gun was destroyed, we jumped into the boats and were carried quickly to safety by the strong current.

CHAPTER XIII

FINAL SERVICE ON THE MISSISSIPPI

UPON the completion of the Red River Expedition, the fleet was again scattered to guard the important communications along the Mississippi River. Except for minor operations the fighting was over, so that Admiral Porter himself returned to Cairo, where he also ordered the *Cairo* to proceed.

The ship proved too slow to make more than about 3 knots against the current, and especially on this account we followed the river custom of taking "cut offs" when proceeding up stream, which of course led into comparatively shallow water. It should be understood that the constant changes of the channels in the Mississippi render its navigation very difficult, and a specialty in itself. Naval captains had to rely upon the experienced pilots assigned to their ship, and these experts were held responsible for the navigation. It was my constant rule not to interfere with the pilots, who were necessarily much better qualified to con the ship than any one else could be. During the trip north the *Osage's* pilots were handicapped from not having been up river for more than a year, and consequently they were not entirely familiar with the changes that had meantime occurred in the river channels. This circumstance led to the *Osage* going aground while attempting a short cut across a large bend.

A line was run to the bank and we did our best in other ways to refloat her, but all efforts were unavailing. The falling river gave every promise of detaining the *Osage* on the shoal for several months, consequently I took the first available transport up river and reported the condition of affairs to Admiral Porter. He relieved me from command of the stranded gunboat, and gave me the newly completed *Vindicator* in her place.

Capable of 16 knots up stream and 20 down, the fastest ship of any type on the river, the fine large ram *Vindicator* was a delight to her new commander, who soon sailed with her for Vicksburg, under orders to take charge of the district between that point and the mouth of the Red River. As we passed the *Osage* I could not restrain a chuckle of self-congratulation, on observing dry land all about her, and a bucket line of men out on the shoal passing water to the ship! Manifestly she could not budge for months. In fact she was not finally refloated until February, after a detention of six months.

On the new station two iron-clads and three or four gunboats, together with the *Vindicator,* comprised my little squadron. In addition to the ordinary duty of protecting river traffic, a special mission was to prevent any crossing of rebel troops. The advance of General Sherman in the vicinity of Atlanta, opposed only by an inferior army under General Hood, had made the Confederates very anxious to reinforce Hood by the army of our late Red River antagonist, General Taylor. The latter was more likely to attempt a crossing in my district than in any other, and I made every effort to prevent it, notwithstanding any probable massing of artillery at a chosen point to cover the passage of the troops.

Selecting those stretches of the river which, on account of natural conditions, were most likely to be chosen for a crossing, the principal naval forces were concentrated there. Each group contained light gunboats backed up by iron-clads in between, while the *Vindicator* cruised rapidly back and forth constantly prepared to reinforce any threatened point. It was very gratifying later on to intercept correspondence which proved the efficacy of these arrangements. One of the captured letters to a friend in Mississippi ran to the following effect:

"DEAR JACK,

"We have been lying in the bottoms behind the levee for two weeks, but are unable to cross because the Yankee gunboats are thicker than fiddlers in hell."

In the course of time Sherman's victorious advance eastward reflected quiet in the affairs on the river, and I had the pleasing prospect, after several years of most strenuous campaigning, of enjoying leisure and recreation in Vicksburg and Natchez, where the social life was very agreeable. Meanwhile, after the gunboat successes on the Cumberland and Tennessee Rivers, operations on the upper Mississippi also settled down to an inactive status, and Admiral Porter received orders to take command of the blockade on the North Atlantic coast of the Confederacy. The writer was acquainted with this prospective change by the receipt of a letter from the Admiral, which closed by saying that if I wanted any more fighting I had better go along with him.

As a matter of fact I was not keen for any more fighting. Three years of constant active service in the face of the enemy had dulled my ardor for adventure, and sharpened my taste for more reposeful pleasures. On the other hand, the compliment of having the Admiral want me with him on the new station, was a spur to continued effort, and moreover the call of duty, to serve where needed, could not be denied. Admiral Porter was told that I would be very glad to go with him to the Atlantic.

By no means the least of the many professional benefits which I had derived from service on the Mississippi, was the stimulating influence of close association with such a fine officer and outstanding personality as Admiral Porter. He had the two most necessary attributes of a war commander—firmness of character and resourcefulness in difficulties. These in combination with high professional attainments, great personal courage, untiring energy, and coolness in battle, made him one of the greatest of our Admirals.

In addition he had the too rare gift of inspiring the loyalty and best endeavors of his subordinates. A general attitude which contributed to this is well illustrated by the incident of the loss of the *Cairo*. The circumstance of my falling in with the flagship *Black Hawk* and going on board to make a report of the accident, has been previously related. It was my first acquaintance with the Admiral. My account of the sinking of one of his best gunboats ended by the remark, "I suppose, Admiral, you will order a Court of Inquiry." This being the procedure prescribed by regulations, the writer had assumed it would follow in his case, as a matter of course. But Porter replied, "Court! I have no time to order courts; I can't blame an officer who seeks to put his ship close to the enemy. Is there any other vessel you would like to have?" My response was to the effect that, there being no vacancy in the command of any vessel except the wooden gunboat *Conestoga,* I would like to have her. Turning to his Fleet Captain, Lieutenant-Commander K. R. Breese, the Admiral said, "Make out Selfridge's orders to the *Conestoga.*" I left with great admiration for a man who could act so promptly and justly, and with a sense of obligation to him that could never be forgotten. Such feelings animated all his subordinates, from his being always ready to recognize and reward merit.

Finally, the charm of Porter's personality played no small part in his military success. His hospitality was unbounded, and his bonhomie and sense of humor made him a delightful companion, which served to inspire all with unshakable loyalty to him personally. Such were the attributes that dominated the organization of the great Mississippi River Fleet, and its brilliant conduct in the face of notable difficulties. In Admiral Porter's death (1891) the Country lost a hero, his family an affectionate husband and father, and myself a very dear comrade.

CHAPTER XIV

WITH PORTER IN THE ATLANTIC

THE journey by rail from Cairo to Washington afforded some little excitement to those on my train. Just ahead of us another train had been held up and burned by Colonel Mosby's guerillas, then engaged in a raid in West Virginia, and there seemed a probability that we would share the same fate. The writer tried to organize a defense among the passengers, who comprised a large proportion of military and naval men, but the lack of any arms, except a few revolvers, prevented adequate response. Just as we approached the vicinity of the holdup, the whistle sounded for the brakes and the train came to a stop, and not relishing a trip to Libby Prison, I quickly sought the shelter of the bushes by the roadside. It developed, however, that the stop had been made only to clear the track of some débris left from the previously destroyed train, and without further adventure, we proceeded to Washington. It was during this visit to the capital that the Secretary of the Navy, Mr. Gideon Welles, was told of the lucky shot in Hampton

Roads early in the war, and he initiated proceedings for the prize money, which has been mentioned before, as due me from the capture of the tug known as the *America*.

A few days later, at Hampton Roads, Admiral Porter handed me orders to command the *Huron*. She was one of those vessels known as "Ninety-day gunboats," from the fact of having been constructed hastily within that short period. Although capable of only 9 knots speed, they mounted one 11-inch gun on pivot, a 30 lb. Parrott on the forecastle, and several brass howitzers, a powerful battery for craft of only about 700 tons displacement, and performed very useful service in the war. The *Huron* being absent up the James River, I awaited her return while quartered temporarily on the *Malvern*, a converted merchantman which the Admiral was using for his flagship.

One afternoon an incident occurred which from a personal viewpoint transcended even the many exciting experiences that had fallen to my lot during the war. Mrs. Porter was visiting the Admiral on board, and in her honor, General Shepley, commanding the forces in the vicinity of Norfolk, together with his family and friends, called to pay their respects, bringing with them a military band. The occasion developed into a tea and dance, but not knowing any of the guests I avoided the party, until accosted on deck by the Fleet Captain, Breese, who urged me to join in the festivities in the cabin below. In spite of some reluctance, I was persuaded to do so, much to my subsequent delight, since the attractions of one of General Shepley's daughters defied indifference.

Upon the arrival of the *Huron* several days afterwards, her boilers were in such bad repair that she was sent to the Navy Yard at Norfolk, for a three weeks overhaul. Naturally I took advantage of the circumstance to renew my acquaintance with Miss Shepley, which resulted in our engagement and, as will appear later, in our marriage during the August immediately following the war.

The first active service of the *Huron* under my command, was a period of several weeks spent blockading the mouth of the Cape Fear River. Fort Fisher guarded what was known as the New Inlet, but our station was to the west of Old Inlet; the usual entrance of blockade runners, guided by the lighthouse at Bald Head, left burning by the Confederates for that purpose. The blockading forces were disposed in a semicircle about this entrance, each vessel covering an arc of approximately two points. It was really extraordinary how easily the blockade runners evaded our forces. Frequently in the afternoon, we would see them drop down the river over the bar and anchor near the lighthouse, but in the morning they would be gone, without our having even sighted them again. Long experience on the blockade had developed a plan by which the faster Federal vessels maintained a position well offshore, in the daylight zone through which blockade runners must pass after a night's run from port. It was here that most of the captures were made.

In December, 1864, Porter assembled his great fleet off Fort Fisher, preliminary to the capture of that place in co-operation with the army, operating from the land side. This affair is described below, in extracts from an article by the writer, published in *Battles and Leaders of the Civil War* (1888).

" . . . The naval command of the expedition having been declined by Admiral Farragut, on account of ill-health, Rear-Admiral Porter, who had so successfully co-operated with the army in opening the Mississippi, was selected, and was allowed to bring with him five of his officers, of whom the writer was one, being detailed for the command of the gunboat *Huron.* The Atlantic and Gulf coasts being almost entirely in our possession, the Navy Department was able to concentrate before Fort Fisher a larger force than had ever before assembled under one command in the history of the American navy—a total of nearly 60 vessels, of which five were iron-clads, including the *New Ironsides,* besides the three largest of our steam-frigates, viz., the *Minnesota, Colorado,* and *Wabash.* The fleet arrived in sight of the fort on the morning of December 20th.

"A novel feature of this first attack was the explosion of a powder-boat near the fort on the night of December 23rd. The vessel was the *Louisiana,* an old gunboat no longer serviceable. The more sanguine believed that Fort Fisher, with its garrisons, guns, and equipment, would be leveled to the ground, while others were equally certain it would prove a fizzle. Commander A. C. Rhind, with a crew of volunteers, successfully performed the perilous duty, and, applying the match at midnight, the crew rowed safely away to the *Wilderness,* a swift gunboat, in waiting. The whole fleet having moved offshore, under low steam, awaited the result with anxiety. A glare on the horizon and a dull report were the indications that the floating mine had been sprung. In the morning, when the fleet steamed in, all eyes were toward the fort. . . . There it was, as grim as ever, apparently uninjured, with its flag floating as defiantly as before. In these days with better electrical appliances, the explosion could have been made more nearly instantaneous, but I doubt if the general result would have been different.

"The powder-boat proving an ignominious failure, the fleet stood in toward the fort in close order of divisions, the iron-clads leading. At 11:30 the signal was thrown out from the flag-ship *Malvern;* 'Engage the enemy.' The *Ironsides,* followed by the monitors, took position as close in as their draught would permit, engaging the north-east face. The *Ironsides* was followed by the *Minne-*

sota, Colorado, and *Wabash.* The enemy replied briskly, but when these frigates found the range and commenced firing rapidly nothing could withstand their broadsides of twenty-five 9-inch guns. It was a magnificent sight to see these frigates fairly engaged, and one never to be forgotten. Their sides seemed a sheet of flame, and the roar of their guns like a mighty thunderbolt. Meanwhile all the other ships took positions as detailed, and so perfect were the plans of the admiral, and so well were they carried out by his captains, that not a mishap took place. Nothing could withstand such a storm of shot and shell as was now poured into this fort. The enemy took refuge in their bomb-proofs, replying sullenly with an occasional gun. The enemy's fire being silenced, signal was made to fire with deliberation, and attention was turned to the dismounting of the guns. So quickly had the guns at Fort Fisher been silenced that not a man had been injured by their fire, though several ships had sustained losses by the bursting of their 100-pounder Parrott rifles. The *Mackinaw,* however, had had her boiler exploded by a shot, and several of her crew had been scalded, and the *Osceola* was struck by a shell near her magazine, but was saved from sinking by her captain, Commander Clitz.

"During the bombardment the transports, with troops, arrived from Beaufort. On Christmas day, as agreed upon between Admiral Porter and General Butler, the smaller vessels were engaged in covering the disembarkation of the troops, while the iron-clads and frigates were sent in to resume the bombardment of the fort. The larger portion of the army was landed by the boats of the fleet and advanced with little or no opposition to within a short distance of the fort, and skirmish-line within fifty yards. Butler and Weitzel decided however that it could not be taken by assault. Orders were issued to re-embark after being on shore but a few hours. Some seven hundred men were left on shore, the sea being too rough to get them off, but the demoralized enemy did not attempt to attack them. They were taken off in the morning, and the transports steamed away for Hampton Roads, the fleet returning to Beaufort. Thus ended the first attack upon Fort Fisher. Words cannot express the bitter feeling and chagrin of the navy. We all felt the fruit was ripe for plucking and with little exertion would have fallen into the hands of the army.

"Second Attack Upon Fort Fisher

"Upon receiving Admiral Porter's dispatches, Mr. Welles again sought the co-operation of the army, to which General Grant at once acceded, sending back the same force of white troops, re-enforced by two colored brigades under General Charles J. Paine, the whole under the command of

Major-General Alfred H. Terry. While lying at Beaufort, Admiral Porter determined to assist in the land attack of the army by an assault upon the sea-face of Fort Fisher with a body of seamen. In a general order volunteers from the fleet were called for, and some two thousand officers and men offered themselves for this perilous duty.

"General Terry arrived off Beaufort with his forces on the 8th of January, 1865, a plan of operations was agreed upon, and the 12th was fixed for the sailing of the combined force.

"Upon the morning of the 13th the iron-clads were sent in to engage the fort. Going in much closer than before, the monitors were within twelve hundred yards of the fort. Their fire was in consequence much more effective.

"The remainder of the fleet were occupied till 2 P.M. in landing the troops and stores. This particular duty, the provisioning of the army, and the protection of its flank was afterward turned over to the lighter gunboats, whose guns were too small to employ them in the bombardment of the fort, the whole under the charge of Commander J. H. Upshur, commanding the gunboat *A. D. Vance.*

"On the afternoon of the 13th the fleet, excepting the iron-clads, which had remained in their first positions close to the fort, steamed into the several positions assigned them and opened a terrific fire. By placing a buoy close to the outer reef, as a guide, the leading ship, the *Minnesota,* was enabled to anchor nearer, and likewise the whole battle-line was much closer and their fire more effective, the best proof of which is the large number of guns upon the land-face of the fort that was found to be destroyed or dismounted. The weight of fire was such that the enemy could make but a feeble reply. At nightfall the fleet hauled off, excepting the iron-clads which kept up a slow fire through the night.

"During the 14th a number of the smaller gun-boats carrying 11-inch guns were sent in to assist in dismounting the guns on the land-face. Their fire was necessarily slow, and the presence of these small craft brought the enemy out of their bomb-proofs to open upon them, during which the *Huron* had her main-mast shot away.[1] Upon seeing this

---

[1] The topmast having been previously 'housed," the rigging between it and the lower-mast prevented the latter from coming down on deck, though suspended at an angle of some forty degrees from the vertical. On this account a number of men were probably saved from injury.

At this time the *Huron's* hull was also hit by an 8-inch shell which, had it exploded, doubtless would have put the vessel out of action. Fortunately the shell had lost most of its initial velocity, and as it approached the ship, tumbling badly, could be clearly seen. Turning to the Executive Officer the writer remarked "That shell seems to be coming straight for us." A moment later it imbedded itself in the *Huron's* side, with its axis fore and aft. Had the impact been nearly perpendicular to the side, the ordinary operation of the fuse probably would have exploded the shell and wrecked the small ship.

After the battle the writer directed the extraction of the shell, hoping to preserve it as a memento of the war. But, like the *Cumberland's* flag, Fate seemed to ordain otherwise. The projectile was so heavy, and so awkward to handle from its position, that it dropped overboard and was never recovered.

renewal of fire, the *Brooklyn, Mohican,* and one or two other vessels were ordered in by Porter, and with this re-enforcement the fire of the fort slackened. The bombardment from the smaller gunboats and iron-clads was kept up during the night. This constant duty day and night was very hard upon these small vessels, and the officers and crew of my own vessel, the *Huron,* were worn out.

"Fort Fisher was at this time much stronger than at the first attack. The garrison had been re-enforced by veteran troops, damages by the first bombardment had been repaired, and new defenses added; among which was a battery of light pieces in a half-moon around the sally-port, from whose fire the sailors suffered heavily in their assault.

"It was arranged that the grand bombardment should begin on the morning of the 15th, and the separate assaults of soldiers and sailors should take place at 3 P. M. A code of signals was agreed upon between the two commanders, and the assault was to be signaled to the fleet by a blowing of steam-whistles, whereupon their fire would be directed to the upper batteries. After the assault of the sailors had failed the *Ironsides* used her 11-inch guns with great effect in firing into the traverses filled with Confederates resisting the advance of the Union forces. At 9 A.M. the fleet was directed by signal to move in three divisions, and each ship took its prescribed place as previously indicated to her commander.

"All felt the importance of this bombardment, and while not too rapid to be ineffective such a storm of shell was poured into Fort Fisher, that forenoon, as I believe had never been seen before in any naval engagement. The enemy soon ceased to make any reply from their heavy guns, excepting the 'Mound Battery,' which was more difficult to silence, while those mounted on the land-face were by this time disabled.

"Before noon the signal was made for the assaulting column of sailors and marines to land. From thirty-five of the sixty ships of the fleet boats shoved off, making, with their flags flying as they pulled toward the beach in line abreast, a most spirited scene. The general order of Admiral Porter required that the assaulting column of sailors should be armed with cutlasses and pistols. It was also intended that trenches or covered ways should be dug for the marines close to the fort and that our assault should be made under the cover of their fire; but it was impossible to dig such shelter trenches near enough to do much good under fire in broad daylight.

"The sailors as they landed from their boats were a heterogeneous assembly, companies of two hundred or more from each of the larger ships, down to small parties of twenty each from the gunboats. They had been for months confined on shipboard, had never drilled together and their arms, the old-fashioned cutlass and pistol, were hardly the weapons to cope with the rifles and bayonets of the enemy. Sailor-like, however, they looked upon the landing in the light of a lark, and few thought the sun would set with a loss of one-fifth of their number.

"After some discussion between the commander, Lieutenant-Commander K. R. Breese, and the senior officers, it was decided to form three divisions, each composed of the men from the corresponding division squadrons of the fleet; the first division, under the command of Lieutenant-Commander C. H. Cushman, the second under Lieutenant-Commander James Parker (who was Breese's senior but waived his rank, the latter being in command as the admiral's representative), the third under Lieutenant-Commander T. O. Selfridge, Jr., a total of 1,600 bluejackets, to which was added a division of 400 marines under Captain L. L. Dawson.

"The whole force marched up the beach and lay down under its cover just outside rifle range, awaiting the movements of the army. We were formed by the flank, and our long line flying numerous flags gave a formidable appearance from the fort, and caused the Confederates to divide their forces, sending more than one-half to oppose the naval assault.

"At a preconcerted signal the sailors sprang forward to the assault, closely following the water's edge, where the inclined beach gave them a slight cover. We were opened upon in front by the great mound battery, and in flank by the artillery of the half-moon battery, and by the fire of a thousand rifles. Though many dropped rapidly under this fire, the column never faltered, and when the angle where the two faces of the fort unite was reached the head halted to allow the rear to come up. This halt was fatal, for as the others came up they followed suit and lay down till the space between the parapet and the edge of the water was filled. As the writer approached with the Third Division he shouted to his men to come on, intending to lead them to where there was more space; but, looking back, he discovered that his whole command, with few exceptions, had stopped and joined their comrades. Making his way to the front, close to the palisade, he found several officers, among whom were Lieutenant-Commanders Parker and Cushman. The situation was a very grave one. The rush of the sailors was over; they were packed like sheep in a pen, while the enemy was crowding the ramparts not forty yards away, and shooting into them as fast as they could fire. There was nothing to reply with but pistols. Something must be done, and speedily. There were some spaces in the palisade where it was torn away by the fire of the fleet, and an attempt was made to charge through, but we found a deep impassable ditch, and those who got through were shot down. Flesh and blood could not long endure being killed in this slaughter-pen, and the rear of the sailors broke, followed by the whole body, in spite of all efforts to rally them.[1] It was certainly mortifying, after charging for a mile, under a most galling fire, to the very foot of the fort, to have the whole force retreat down the beach. It has been the custom, unjustly in my opinion, to lay the blame on the marines for not keeping down the fire till the sailors could get in. But there were but 400 of them against 1,200 of the garrison; the former in the open plain, and with no cover; the latter under the shelter of their ramparts. The mistake was in expecting a body of sailors, collected hastily from different ships, unknown to each other, armed with swords and pistols, to stand against veteran soldiers armed with rifles and bayonets. Another fatal mistake was the stopping at the sea angle. Two hundred yards farther would have brought us to a low parapet

[1]The writer started back after the panic-stricken men with the object of rallying them, but had taken only a dozen steps when the futility of doing so dawned upon him. Not being willing to participate in the retreat, he threw himself flat on his back in the sand, and squirmed his body to gain what shelter might be afforded from a slight depression thus created. The result was negligible, since the Confederates, only forty yards away, were firing downwards from high ramparts, and nothing further could be done but to lie as still as possible in the hope that they might assume me to be dead or wounded. A moment after my seeking safety in this way, Captain Breese walked near, on his way to the front after vainly endeavoring to rally the men. I called out to him, advised against the palpable folly of his attempting further aggressive action, and suggested that he join me in the sand. He laid down beside me, and we "played possum" with great care, until the onset of dusk, an hour later, permitted us to join the main forces at the beach.

without palisade or ditch, where, with proper arms, we could have intrenched and fought. Some sixty remained at the front, at the foot of the parapet, under cover of the palisade, until nightfall enabled them to withdraw. Among the number I remember Lieutenant-Commanders Breese, Parker, Cushman, Sicard; Lieutenants Farquhar, Lamson, S. W. Nichols, and Bartlett.

"A loss of some three hundred in killed and wounded attests the gallant nature of the assault. Among these were several prominent officers, including Lieutenants Preston and Porter, killed; Lieutenant-Commanders C. H. Cushman, W. N. Allen, Lieutenant G. M. Bache, wounded.

"After their repulse the sailors did good service with the marines by manning the intrenchments thrown up across the peninsula, which enabled General Terry to send Abbott's brigade and Blackman's (27th U.S.) colored regiment to the assistance of the troops fighting in the fort. Here they remained till morning when they returned to their respective ships. When the assault of the marine column failed, the *Ironsides* and the monitors were directed to fire into the gun traverses in advance of the position occupied by the army, and by doing so greatly demoralized the enemy. About 8 P.M. that night the fort fell into our hands after the hardest fighting by our gallant troops, and with its capture fell the last stronghold of the Southern Confederacy on the Atlantic coast.

"I will not go so far as to say the army could not have stormed Fort Fisher without the diversion afforded by the naval assault, for no soldiers during the war showed more indomitable pluck than the gallant regiments that stormed the fort on that afternoon; but I do say our attack enabled them to get into the fort with far less loss than they would otherwise have suffered.

"As a diversion the charge of sailors was a success; as an exhibition of courage it was magnificent; but the material of which the column was composed, and the arms with which it was furnished, left no reasonable hope after the first onslaught had been checked that it could have succeeded.

"While kept under the walls of the fort, I was an eye-witness of an act of heroism on the part of Assistant-Surgeon William Longshaw, a young officer of the medical staff, whose memory should ever be kept green by his corps, and which deserves more than this passing notice. A sailor too severely wounded to help himself had fallen close to the water's edge, and with the rising tide would have drowned. Dr. Longshaw, at the peril of his life, went to his assistance and dragged him beyond the incoming tide. At this moment he heard a cry from a wounded marine, one of a small group who, behind a little hillock of sand close to the parapet, kept up a fire upon the enemy. Longshaw ran to his assistance, and while attending to his wounds was shot dead. What made the action of this young officer even more heroic was the fact that on that very day he had received a leave of absence, but had postponed his departure to volunteer for the assault."

CHAPTER XV

After the fall of Fort Fisher, Admiral Porter anchored all the small vessels of the fleet, including his flagship, just inside the Cape Fear River. That same night, deceived by the continuance of the Bald Head lighthouse, two blockade runners came in and anchored, not aware of the recent operations. In fact the elation of their crews over what was thought to be another successful run in, led to a jolly celebration, with liberal quantities of wines and liquors, served out to both officers and crew. In the midst of the party, they were greatly surprised by the arrival of Federal boarding officers, who made them prisoners. The cargoes of blockade runners and the ships were Federal property, subject to adjudication by a prize court, but the ordinary mess stores and minor equipment were considered as the legitimate prize of the personnel making the capture. Accordingly, on the following morning, signal was sent to all ships of the fleet for boats to proceed to the prizes, and transfer their large stores of wines to the flagship. But by the time the laden boats had reached that destination a stiff northwest breeze had sprung up, making precarious any further transfer of the fragile cargoes, and the boats were sent back to their respective ships until the following morning. It is needless to say that their final deliveries were short a good many cases of wines, which had found their way on board various ships of the fleet, and which served as inspiration for frequent card parties and other gayeties, during the otherwise inactive two weeks that followed.

A few days after the first two captures, a third blockade runner, the *Dumbarton,* dropped anchor just outside the river not far from the *Huron,* which was signaled to take possession of her. The writer went on board and found her captain much chagrined at being captured in this way, after two years of successful blockade running, notwithstanding that his ship could not make more than 9 knots. Here I made two very useful captures. Knowing that the prize had come from England, I asked the captain if he did not have a Stilton cheese, and he presented me with one of that famous brand. In the same way was obtained a very fine pair of Boudin binoculars, much superior to any then made in the United States. These proved of great utility during my subsequent service in the Navy, and remained in my possession until a few years ago, when they were stolen from my summer house in Jamestown, R. I.

Three weeks of waiting ended by initiating the projected advance up the river to Wilmington, in conjunction with the army. General Schofield cleared the banks, supported by Porter's fleet, which included about a dozen "double-enders"—specially built light draft gunboats, mounting two 11-inch guns, one forward and one aft. Wilmington fell with very little resistance, and most of the fleet, including the *Huron,* then proceeded to the James River, to assist Grant's army in operations which finally brought about the fall of Richmond.

When the Confederacy collapsed, its President, Jefferson Davis, escaped from Virginia, and it was suspected that his destination might be overseas. The coast being well guarded, except about Florida, Admiral Porter received instructions to send some light draft gunboats to that vicinity, but of all the great number of such vessels comprising his fleet, the *Huron* was the only one sufficiently fit to undertake the service. We reached Key West safely, notwithstanding the possibility of being captured by the Confederate steamer *Stonewall,* then at Havana, only to learn that Jefferson Davis had been taken prisoner in northern Georgia. Consequently Commodore Stribling, then commanding at Key West, instructed me to proceed to New York.

On this, the last voyage of the *Huron* during the war, the salting up of her boilers caused much trouble. Gradually the best speed was reduced to about 3 knots, and finally when off Cape Hatteras, with a northeast gale brewing, the chief engineer reported that he could make no steam at all. I said to him, "Chief, what do you propose doing?" He replied that, if the ship could be stopped for forty-eight hours, he would draw fires from the boilers, clean the salt from the crown sheets which were dropping, and from the tubes, and then he believed we could reach our destination. While repairs were in progress there was no alternative but to anchor, which involved great danger of being blown upon a dangerous lee shore, in the probable event of bad weather. We had only the two bower anchors and a stream anchor. I concluded that the arrangement to give the best promise of holding in a gale, was to shackle together the two bower cables, and to back the bower anchor with the stream. Veering to a scope of 200 fathoms of chain, the ship rode very easily through the severe northeast gale that followed, while the salt was removed from the boilers. Without further incident we were then able to make New York, where the ship was placed out of commission.

Thus ended my service in the great Civil War. It had been four long years of extremely arduous work, involving constant danger and a number of hairbreadth escapes, from which I was most fortunate in being spared with scarcely a scratch. Years afterwards (in 1881) it was exceedingly gratifying to learn from Admiral Porter, that a board of

Admirals of which he was a member, meeting shortly after the close of the war, had recommended me for a promotion of thirty numbers on the Navy List, in recognition of my war services. The compliment was enhanced by the fact that only three other officers (Rhind, Jouett, and Bache) were nominated for this, the maximum reward permitted by law, and that in my case the vote of the board had been unanimous, on account of "conspicuous gallantry in battle."

But notwithstanding such a recommendation, from contemporaries whose character, judgment, and abilities, had been amply demonstrated while exercising high command in the crucible of war, no promotions resulted from the board's action. It was not the custom at that period to reward naval officers with medals or promotion, except by special act of Congress. This was done for eminent men like Farragut, and Porter, and others. Political influence resulted in legislation which promoted other officers besides these, for conspicuous service. But for the Navy as a whole, Congress very wisely concluded that selections for such reward should be made only by a board of officers. A law was passed, authorizing promotion within a limit of thirty numbers, and the Secretary accordingly ordered the selection board referred to above, comprising the most successful commanders of the late naval operations; of course including Admirals Farragut and Porter. Secretary Welles, however, pigeon-holed its report, notwithstanding a general conviction that the recommendation of such a well-qualified body of officers should be followed in promoting the most deserving, from among the many who had fought so gallantly during a great crisis in the life of the nation.[1]

I have no means of knowing the reasoning which prompted Secretary Welles in his negative action. Perhaps he was fearful of risking adverse effects upon the morale of the officer body as a whole, at a time when post war readjustments were already straining such morale. Undoubtedly this is an objection to a system of rewarding officers for war service after the war has been terminated. On the other hand, some hope of reward for conspicuous service, is an element in the success of naval and military hostilities too valuable to neglect. Our laws should be so framed that medals and promotions, when deserved, may be given immediately after the event; of course only on recommendation of the commanders at the front, who alone are

[1] Many years afterwards I was very much gratified to receive the following letter from Captain F. M. Bunce, containing an opinion of Secretary Welles as to my war service:—

U. S. Naval Training Station,
Newport, R. I., May 30, 1922.

Captain Thos. O. Selfridge, U. S. Navy,
My dear Selfridge:

You ask for a statement of an opinion of your war record given by the late Secretary of the Navy Gideon Welles to me.

The circumstances were, that on the completion of the voyage of the *Monadnock* from Philadelphia to San Francisco in 1866, under my command, on the recommendation of Commodore John

capable of estimating the relative difficulty and value of the various services rendered.

After the Spanish War the Department wisely changed its policy respecting rewards. For service in that war, some officers and men were promoted, some received special medals, and all participants were given so called "campaign medals." Subsequently it was decided to issue campaign medals to participants in previous wars, and in 1908 I received such a campaign medal of the general type designated for Civil War service. But no reward within the power of the Navy Department, could give me as much satisfaction as was derived from the following letter.

"WASHINGTON, D. C.,
"November 23, 1874.

"MY DEAR SIR:

"No one can tell in this world how soon his mortal career may be ended and one should not put off till tomorrow what can be done today.

Rodgers, the Secretary wished to promote me a grade, and he stated to me that he regretted he could not do so because on examination he found that there were three officers, yourself, Geo. H. Perkins, and Edward Terry of my grade, and above me on the list, whose war records were as good or better than mine,—that he thought your war record to be unexcelled by that of any officer in the Navy except Farragut.

No action was taken, and I have never regretted the fact, feeling satisfied with the reason given and the compliment to me therein conveyed.

Sincerely yours,

F. M. BUNCE.

"I often feel that I would like those young officers who served with and supported me during the most important command I held during the war—that of the Mississippi Squadron, to know that I appreciated all their zeal and ability.

"I take advantage of a leisure moment to write you a few lines which although they will bring you no advancement will I am sure gratify you when you look back to past events and you and others I hope will not fail to remember that I always gave the credit of my victories to the officers who served under me.

"I think you will find yourself mentioned as frequently if not oftener than any other officer who went into battle under my command.

"If war should come before I get to be an old fogy or broken down by age you may rest assured that I shall have you near me and am satisfied that you will make as good a record as in the past.

"Before a great while you will have passed the thirty-five numbers that obstruct the way to a captaincy and will come before the Board for examination. You can show them this letter and say to the members that had the recommendations of the Board of Admirals, of which I was a member, been carried out you would have been a captain before the year 1874.

"You can console yourself with the reflection that you earned your promotion even if an unjust head of the Department withheld it, and that it was awarded to you by a board of officers who had led the squadrons of the Navy.

"You have I hope a long and successful career before you and go where you will you have the best wishes of

"Yours very sincerely,
"DAVID D. PORTER,
"Admiral.

"Commander
"THOMAS O. SELFRIDGE,
"U. S. N."

CHAPTER XVI

ON detachment from the *Huron,* I received orders to report as executive officer of the *Hartford,* then about to proceed to China. Having been almost continuously at sea during my entire naval service of eleven years, since graduating from the Naval Academy, and the last four years having been active war service, it seemed rather an undue hardship to embark on a new cruise which promised three more years on a distant foreign station. The outlook was particularly displeasing on account of my prospective marriage. In these circumstances I went to Washington and acquainted Admiral Porter with my dilemma. He was kind enough to intercede in my behalf, and had me ordered to the Naval Academy, where he was going as Superintendent.

During the war, the Academy had been moved to Newport, and the buildings at Annapolis used as hospitals, to receive the numerous wounded incident to Grant's heavy fighting in Virginia. While these buildings were being again made ready for the use of Midshipmen, I obtained leave, during which my marriage to Miss Shepley took place in the month of August, 1865. On September 1st a three year tour of duty was begun at Annapolis, as an instructor in the Department of Seamanship.

The usual academic work was broken by three annual summer practice cruises, all of which I made on the old *Macedonian*. No special interest attaches to the first cruise along our northeast Atlantic coast in 1866.

The following Summer the practice squadron under Commodore Luce, was sent to Cherbourg to attend the French Exposition, and on the trip over the *Savannah* and *Dale* remained in company with the flagship *Macedonian*. The poor sailing qualities of the *Dale,* however, so delayed the progress of the squadron as a whole, that for the return voyage the Commodore allowed each ship to proceed independently. Of course this meant a race, especially between ourselves and the *Savannah* which was slightly faster than the *Macedonian*. The other two ships of the squadron chose the route home by way of the trades, while I selected the more stormy northern passage where favorable winds were more doubtful, though stronger winds more prevalent. It caused me no little satisfaction, after crowding on sail all the way, to arrive home ten days ahead of the *Savannah*. The little *Dale* was a month behind us, so late that her midshipmen had no leave that Summer!

This homeward passage furnished a yarn about Captain Dick Meade of the *Dale,* who was something of a "Tartar." Becoming impatient while becalmed, he ordered his executive, Lieutenant O'Kane, to get out all boats and tow the ship! After four hours of this, Captain Meade came on deck and asked, "Mr. O'Kane, how much speed are you making?" O'Kane, who was quite a wit, pointed to a chip in the water and replied, "Do you see that chip over there, sir? It has been in sight all the watch." The towing evolution ended then and there.

For the summer cruise of 1868, to the Azores and Madeira, Commodore Luce chose the *Savannah* as his flagship, and the *Macedonian* accompanied her during the outward passage; the former's small margin of speed usually requiring us to carry a topmast studdingsail to keep up. Before leaving Madeira, I asked Luce to permit the *Macedonian* to proceed independently, so as to beat the *Savannah* home. He replied that the *Macedonian* was not fast enough, but nevertheless granted the request for a race.

The two ships left Madeira together, the *Savannah* taking the more southerly route through the trade belt, while we crossed in about Latitude 25°. The *Macedonian* carried a cloud of canvas in all but heavy weather, a lower studdingsail being fitted on the main, a spare jib carried as a staysail, and even a main skysail rigged. This was the first time I had ever known a skysail to be carried on a man-of-war, and though it really had very little value in increasing the speed of the ship, it added to the interest of the race. My night orders were to keep the skysail set unless the ship logged more than 7 knots, but even at this speed the temporary rig stood up so well, that finally it was left to the discretion of the officer of the deck when he should take in the lofty sail.

We had a quick passage; my recollection is that the Capes of Virginia were sighted after twenty-two days, and here all hands eagerly scanned the horizon for a glimpse of the *Savannah* to learn the outcome of the race. Crowds of midshipmen spent most of the day aloft for this purpose, but with no reward, and we greatly feared that she might be ahead of us. Near Cape Henry we took on board a pilot named Fowler, who had long served practice ships, and as he climbed over the gangway, my first question was, "Fowler, has the *Savannah* arrived yet?" On his replying in the negative a great cheer went up all over the ship.

However the race was not won until we had beaten her into port, and favored by a fresh southerly wind, we crowded on as much sail as possible for the run up Chesapeake Bay. On approaching Annapolis the pilot advised against going in until high tide, but fearful that the strong breeze might bring the *Savannah* in sight at any moment, and being very familiar with Annapolis harbor, I took issue with the pilot and expressed the opinion that there was sufficient water on the bar. He replied that he knew where the best depths could be found, and that if I would take the responsibility he would make the attempt. This being agreed upon, we headed in. As the ship crossed the bar we could feel her bump repeatedly, but finally she scraped over, and standing in under all sail, we came to, smartly, off the Santee wharf at about 10 A.M., by simultaneously backing the topsails, taking in the light sails, and dropping anchor. That very day, before 6 P. M., the *Savannah* hove in sight with a "bone in her teeth," but by that time the *Macedonian's* sails had been furled, and the yards nicely squared, and as far as outward appearance went, one might have thought she had been there a week. The relatively deep draft of the *Savannah* detained her outside the bar for several days, correspondingly postponing the leave of her midshipmen, while ours had departed in great glee immediately after arrival.

Three years of very pleasant duty at the Naval Academy were terminated in 1868, by orders to command the *Nipsic,* a steam gunboat attached to the Home Squadron. The first few months were spent in Cuban waters, where the monotony of ordinary peace cruising was relieved by two unusual incidents. At Cienfuegos I received a visit from a young American engineer in great mental distress. He was in love with, and wished to marry, an attractive Cuban girl, but, apparently on account of the prevalent Spanish prejudice against persons from the north of the United States, growing out of our but recently concluded Civil War, the local Spanish priest refused to perform the wedding ceremony. Much to the delight of the young couple, I came to the rescue by personally officiating in marrying them the next day on board the *Nipsic,* in the presence of the other officers assembled in service uniform. Immediately afterwards the wardroom officers were hosts at a wedding breakfast, following which the bride and groom went ashore filled with gratitude and happiness. The fact of this uncommon incident was noted in the ship's log, a certified copy of the entry given to the groom, and another copy sent to the State Department. I felt legally justified in assisting these young people because of the statutes of several of our states, which authorized a commissioned officer of the United States to conduct a wedding.

Shortly after this affair the *Nipsic* went to Trinidad, Cuba, and there Spanish prejudice took a different turn in the refusal of the local customs officials to clear an American barque, recently loaded with sugar. Her captain appealed to me to expedite the matter, and by him I sent word to the American Consul to inform the Collector of Customs that, unless the ship was promptly cleared, I would take possession of the customs house and tow her out of port. This had the necessary effect. The essential papers were soon issued, but in order to anticipate possible further interference with her departure, through the local official communicating with Havana, I got the *Nipsic* under way and towed the barque to sea. Long afterwards, while dining with an old friend in Boston, I learned by accident that he was part owner of the vessel. He was most grateful to me for the assistance which had been rendered at Trinidad.

Within a few months, orders were received for the *Nipsic* to make a confidential reconnaissance of the coasts of Santo Domingo and Haiti, with a view to the selection of a site for a United States naval base, which President Grant hoped to acquire in that vicinity through subsequent diplomatic action.

En route to Haiti, one night while steaming through the Old Bahama Channel against the prevailing trade wind, the engines suddenly stopped. Leaving my cabin for the deck, I was informed that the engines could not be made to turn over, and, assuming that a water-logged tree or piece of wreckage had been jammed in the propeller, I directed that a man be sent down the stern jacob's ladder to inspect. Great was my surprise to learn that the propeller was gone, having dropped off when the main shaft broke at an unsuspected flaw.

It was a confusing sensation, to have the ship suddenly transformed from a handy steamer into an awkward sailing vessel, especially in the narrow channel where fresh steady winds blew from a direction precisely opposite to the desired course. However there was no alternative but to make sail without delay, and after mentally debating whether to take the fair wind back to the United States, since the accident rendered it almost impossible for the confidential mission to be accomplished in the *Nipsic,* I finally decided to beat through the channel and proceed to Port au Prince. There the situation was explained to the Senior Officer Present, Captain Irwin, who ordered the ship to return to Washington.

Great disappointment over the failure of the expedition moved me to prepare, during the passage north, a report on the advantages of Mole St. Nicholas for naval purposes. Its strategic position, close to the Windward Passage, was exceptionally good, and from the chart the tactical assets of a landlocked harbor protected by high hills, together with an anchorage area sufficiently commodious for a dozen or more vessels of that day, could be well demonstrated. This carefully prepared report was submitted on arrival at Washington, and had an amusing sequel.

At the first opportunity I called to pay my respects upon Admiral Porter, then serving as the principal advisor to the Secretary of the Navy, whose office was in the adjoining room. The Admiral took me in to meet the new Secretary,

Mr. George M. Robeson, who had assumed office but a few days previously, and who had not yet accustomed himself to the status of a Cabinet Officer. My innate awe, common to most young naval officers in the presence of the Secretary of the Navy, was thrown "off center" by a cordial democratic "man to man" greeting. The Secretary had just finished reading my newly received report on Mole St. Nicholas, which he thought excellent and so valuable that he intended placing it before a pending Cabinet meeting at the White House! He wished me to dine with him that evening at the old Wormley Hotel and discuss the matter!

Expressions of appreciation of his kindness left the way open to him gracefully to avoid confirming the invitation to dinner, which under the circumstances seemed an unnecessary imposition upon him. Nevertheless he insisted, not only on my acceptance, but also on knowing my favorite wine. I replied, "You are very kind, Mr. Secretary, but a young naval officer cannot afford to have a favorite wine; whatever kind you may order will be very agreeable to me." "No," he said, "you must have some preference, and I want to order it for you." I could do nothing less than admit to a special fondness for Burgundy.

At dinner that evening I was the only guest, and a quart bottle of Burgundy awaited me at the opposite end of the table from the Secretary's bottle of Madeira. Mr. Robeson proved to be a very delightful host, and my sense of uncomfortable restraint was soon dissipated by his affability. However, Burgundy being rather too heady for my habits, towards the end of the dinner I could feel its effects, and somewhat alarmed over the possibility of intoxication in such circumstances, I started to say good night so soon as the proprieties would permit. "You are not going already!" said the genial Secretary, "Why, you have not drunk half your bottle. I won't hear of your going until it is finished, and you must keep me company while I do the same."

There was no escape. It seemed too disrespectful to do otherwise than comply with wishes, which to a young naval officer were the equivalent of orders. The pleasant evening wore on with the wine affecting us both more and more. But finally when the bottles were finished, I was delighted to find myself still able to preserve sufficient poise while making my adieux. However more embarrassments were to come. "It's a long way down to the Navy Yard," said the Secretary, "I'll drive you down in my carriage," and despite my protests he insisted on doing so.

During the long drive to the Yard the wine gradually made us both more jovial than ever. Unfortunately, his limited experience in high office denied him the full enjoyment which I derived from the novel situation, of a young officer being escorted back to his ship at a late hour by the Secretary of the Navy, both of them rather the worse for wear. At the Navy Yard gate, however, I protested successfully against putting my kind host to any further inconvenience, maintaining that it was only a short walk to the ship. Reluctantly he consented to stopping the carriage and letting me out, and as if to make amends for a lack of complete hospitality, slapped me on the shoulder and said with much emphasis, "Mr. Selfridge, if ever you want anything, you just call on George R."

I am glad to testify to sufficient remaining sobriety on my own part to thank him and say good night with due deference, as well as to sufficient subsequent good sense, never to attempt taking advantage of what were manifestly sincere offers of assistance. But I could not help being immensely amused on the occasion of our next meeting, some two years later, when he greeted me at arm's length with all the manner of a conventional Cabinet Officer.

CHAPTER XVII

SURVEYING THE ISTHMUS OF DARIEN

FOLLOWING a period of several months, during which a new type of propeller was installed in the *Nipsic,* and tried out by runs in Chesapeake Bay, orders were received to undertake a survey of the Isthmus of Darien, with a view to the discovery of a possible route for a ship canal between the Atlantic and Pacific Oceans. This subject had greatly interested President Grant, and due to his initiative and influence, Congress had made an appropriation for exploration purposes. The difficulties at Panama, and other more northerly routes, including Nicaragua, were well known, and deemed so insuperable for the engineering facilities of the day, that it was hoped a more practicable route could be found across the almost unknown region of Darien.

The general scope and importance of the work assigned, is indicated by the following extracts from a letter of instructions issued to me by the Secretary of the Navy in January, 1870:

"Sir: You are appointed to the command of an expedition to make a survey of the Isthmus of Darien, to ascertain the point at which to cut a canal from the Atlantic to the Pacific Ocean. The steam sloop *Nipsic* and the storeship *Guard* will be under your immediate command, while a vessel of Rear-Admiral Turner's fleet will be detailed to co-operate with you on the Pacific side.

"The Department has intrusted to you a duty connected with the greatest enterprise of the present age; and upon your enterprise and zeal will depend whether your name is honorably identified with one of the facts of the future.

.   .   .   .   .

"It will be necessary to take every precaution to propitiate the Indians on the Isthmus, who may be made of great service to the expedition. A contrary course might make them very troublesome enemies. . . .

"As it is probable that some of your people will contract the fever of the Isthmus, you will make proper sanitary arrangements, and furnish your command with all the necessaries required in case of sickness. . . .

"Inclosed is a list of observations to be made, geological specimens to be obtained, heights of mountains to be measured, depths of rivers to be sounded, botanical specimens to be procured, etc. Besides this you will obtain a list of the products of the country, and give an account of the climate and character of the people.

"Although the Department has no intention of tying you down to any particular method of proceeding in your reconnaissance, yet it is deemed prudent to furnish you with such information as may serve to guide you in your researches, and to point out difficulties which it is desirable to avoid.

"All the expeditions which have hitherto made a search for a line of low level across the Isthmus of Darien have furnished maps of but little accuracy. Still these maps are useful for letting you know where these expeditions failed, and it would scarcely be worth while to follow in the footsteps of a party that had produced no evidence that a low line of levels was to be found within the area of their explorations. It is well to profit by the failures of others, and a careful investigation of their proceedings may lead to success.

"No matter how many surveys have been made, or how accurate they may be, the people of this country will never be satisfied until every point of the Isthmus is surveyed by some responsible authority, and by properly equipped parties, such as will be under your command, working on properly matured plans.

.   .   .   .   .

"I do not consider that I am doubting your prudence when I again suggest the importance of cultivating the kindest feelings with the natives of the Isthmus. On this depends the success of your expedition. These people are known to be much opposed to strangers gaining a correct knowledge of their country; but by a proper display of kindness they may be won over to consent to such explorations and surveys being made as are necessary, and may ultimately be persuaded to co-operate with you. Whatever friendly feeling they may manifest, the history of the past and their doubtful character should induce you to be at all times on your guard and prepared for any contingency. A proper display of force, ever on the alert, may prevent hostilities which would otherwise occur.

   .   .   .   .   .

"Very respectfully,
"(Signed) George M. Robeson,
"Secretary of the Navy."

The task which had been allotted to me was one of extreme difficulty, and I count its successful accomplishment the most notable of my naval career. Before starting for the Isthmus several months were spent in study of the special problems that would confront us when in the field, and in devising means for their satisfactory solution. Even for a virgin country it was no ordinary surveying expedition. The Secretary's instructions had emphasized the danger of failure inherent in the hostility of the native inhabitants, which had previously balked all except the most haphazard exploration. It was out of the question to consider taking a sufficiently large military force to eliminate this difficulty with certainty. Several thousand soldiers would be required to guarantee security to small scattered survey parties against attacks, and even if such numbers of troops, and the necessary naval accommodations for them could have been obtained, the difficulties of supplying them at remote points, in the interior of a tropical country wholly lacking in roads and transport, would have increased rather than lightened the burdens of the expedition. One company of marines was decided upon as the most suitable military guard for the inland operations.

An even greater danger than that to be expected from the natives, was the notorious unhealthiness of the Isthmus. Of all tropical regions it had the worst reputation for sickness. Provision against this involved proper food and clothing, as well as medicines, camp equipment, mosquito netting, work routine, etc. The excellence of the foresight and preparations is evidenced by the fact that during three successive survey seasons not a single man died from tropical sickness, notwithstanding that frequently more than 150 men were in the field, many of them for two months at a time, exposed to constant wet and the most fatiguing labor.

Next to the military and hygienic protection of the expedition, the most difficult problem to solve was that of supply for the field parties that had to penetrate long distances into the virgin jungle and be separated from the ships for weeks at a time. Their radius of action necessarily would depend upon their food supply, and their ability to transport it in addition to the surveying instruments and camp equipment. To the ordinary difficulties of transportation through rough and unbroken tropical country, would be added an excessive rainfall, even during the so called "dry season," and a lack of assistance by native carriers. I devised a "Darien ration," consisting of hard bread, bacon, beans, and tinned tomato soup packed in small watertight wooden barrels, and this proved eminently satisfactory for the purpose.

The least difficult provision was a variety of surveying and other scientific instruments of ordinary type, but even in this matter special precaution had to be taken against excessive rainfall. For example, a plane-table often proved to be useless from the fact that the record was obliterated, and at times the paper disintegrated, by the rain.

We were to find that in spite of the most careful preparations, the success of the expedition also depended upon extraordinary persistence and willingness to endure hardships. The tropical sun, torrential rains, floods, raging currents, swamps, dense vegetation, poisonous snakes, blood-sucking bats, tarantulas, scorpions, hornets, wildcats, sand flies, and mosquitoes so thick that I have seen them put out a lighted candle with their burnt bodies, all were to test our resolution to the utmost. These were the difficulties which had kept the secrets of the interior of the Isthmus locked up for hundreds of years.

Tardy orders and the need for thorough preparations prevented final departure from New York until late in January, 1870. Machinery trouble, together with stops at Aspinwall and Porto Bello, for repairs and the procurement of native laborers, further delayed arrival in the field until the end of February. This meant that the first year's work must be short, since but half of the dry season remained.

The route between Caledonia Bay, in the Atlantic, and San Miguel Bay, in the Pacific, was chosen for the initial operations. Upon this line in particular we had been led to expect interruptions from the Mountain Indians, and it seemed wiser to combat them while our strength was unimpaired, rather than after our energies and enthusiasm had been diminished by difficulties elsewhere. This route also offered the important advantage of excellent harbors at each end; a condition that could not be so well duplicated by any other possible isthmian transit. The harbor on the Pacific side was the outlet of the Tuyra River, into which flowed the Chucunaque, a large tributary having its headwaters in the hills close to the Atlantic Ocean, and abreast Caledonia Bay. The discovery of a low gap through these hills therefore would prove the practicability of the route, since the river valley through the remainder of the distance to the Pacific necessarily followed a line of low levels.

The probability of a low passage through these hills had been in controversy for many years. Mr. Gisborne, an English engineer, and Lieutenant Strain, U. S. N., had both explored the vicinity and pronounced the route impracticable. But unfortunately the great physical difficulties which they encountered, and the heroic sufferings they endured, prevented them from obtaining conclusive engineering data; and opposed to their opinion was that of Dr. Cullen, who for several years had stoutly maintained the existence of a feasible route through the hills. A map had been forwarded to me, upon which was traced a watercourse that Cullen asserted led from a low divide in the hills, and ended in a main stream near the Atlantic Ocean.

It is important for the reader to understand the intimate relation between watercourses and the main object of the expedition. As a matter of necessity the streams marked the lowest levels in their vicinity, and their upward courses led toward the lowest points in the isthmian divide. This fact, suggested to me by Admiral Ammen, furnished the basis of my whole plan of operations from the beginning, and moved me to limit survey work principally to the determination of levels along rivers and about the points adjacent to their head-waters. More extensive surveying was not only superfluous, but unquestionably also would have resulted in the complete failure of the expedition, from the great extent of the ground and the insuperable difficulties of traversing it.

On February 22nd, the day after arrival at Caledonia Bay, survey parties were landed with orders to locate the mouth of the stream traced by Cullen. Whether or not this was found near the shore line, the hill country where its headwaters were supposed to exist, would have to be explored, and since this district was inhabited by the Indians from whom hostile resistance was expected, an immediate reconnaissance in force was decided upon. Several parleys with the chief of the local coast Indians resulted in his reluctant promise to furnish guides, and early on the 26th I landed with 88 men, including the whole marine guard, several naval officers and sailors, and the "macheteros" brought from Aspinwall. Leaving behind a small survey party to follow up with a pace traverse, the main body proceeded several miles to the rendezvous where the guides were to join. Here, no Indians were to be seen, and at first I thought they had deceived us, but after repeated hallooing by our interpreter, several faces peered out from near-by bushes. Their owners proved to be the guides sent by the old chief to conduct us towards his village.

We were soon introduced to the strange preju-
dices and characteristics common to all tribes of
Darien Indians. They chose the most difficult and
indirect paths, repeatedly crossing a river which
had to be waded breast high. They insisted upon
my going ahead of them alone, well in advance of
the main body, and to prevent losing the way I
had to halt frequently. Finally a stop was put to
their ridiculous mistrust by compelling them to
join the main force and guide us properly. After
marching three hours we met the old chief, who
showed a reluctance to permit us to proceed
farther, so we halted for breakfast. This finished,
the chief was still unwilling to have us advance, but
on being warned that unless he showed us the right
trail toward the mountains, some of the party
might unknowingly stumble upon his village, he
relented, and himself accompanied us until we were
safely by the village.

The basis of the inhospitality and hostility of
these Indians is a dread of strangers violating their
women; a feeling probably perpetuated by the tradition of the days of the Spanish conquerors.
During three seasons of surveying on the Isthmus
I rarely saw an Indian woman. Even when villages were entered accidentally, it was almost in-
variably found that the women had been previously
hidden. It is the universal custom to discourage
visitors from penetrating into the country. Each
community manifests a strong desire to get rid of

them as soon as possible, telling any stories that seem likely to produce such result. The inhabitants of one village will insist that no pass or path exists in their vicinity, but that good ones may be found in other localities, and it may be readily imagined how this peculiarity handicapped our endeavors, even when among peaceful tribes.

The reconnoitering party's first night in camp was decidedly disagreeable. It began to rain hard, and the rapidly rising river soon washed us out of our frail tenements, which had been constructed close to the banks on the supposition that it was the dry season. The morning found us wet and tired, after a sleepless night, in what we dubbed "Rainy Hollow," where the day was spent in resting and waiting for the small survey party to catch up. On the following morning the advance was resumed, though our guides refused to go any farther, and soon we were struggling over a rough and precipitate ridge, in the face of a heavy rain. At one point a stream had to be crossed. The advance waded through knee deep; ten minutes after, when I came up, the waters were breast high, foaming and tearing over the boulders at not less than five miles an hour, but by felling a tree the remainder of the men were able to cross. Four hours of this kind of marching took us over the ridge and to the headwaters of another stream, when the men were so exhausted that we made camp at 3 P.M. Among the party were veteran soldiers who declared that no march during the war had equaled the severity of this one.

We broke camp early the next morning and picked our way laboriously down a faint trail leading from one bank of the stream to the other, over wet and slippery stones. At 11 o'clock fresh tracks of Indians were observed, and on our interpreter calling out, "Nuetti" (friends), a half dozen natives appeared on the opposite bank. This was our first meeting with the notoriously unfriendly mountain tribe, whose conciliation was so important to gain. Halting the column, the writer crossed the stream with the interpreter and, during a short conversation, astonished them by dropping a metallic cartridge into the water, and then firing it from a rifle. They were familiar with fire-arms of an old type, being supplied with shotguns and flint-locks in addition to bows and poisoned arrows, but the demonstration of ammunition which would fire when wet, greatly impressed them. However, they firmly refused the suggestion that I should go to their village, maintaining that the way was far and the trail difficult, so not wishing to alarm them we made camp, after they had promised to bring their chief for an interview the next day.

In the morning a young Indian came to camp and conducted a few officers and myself to a point half a mile down the river, to await the arrival of the chief. Before long, some twenty-five armed Indians appeared on the opposite bank, and I suspected treachery. It was an uncomfortable situation, since our small advance party carried no arms, but there was no choice other than a bold face, and our fears were happily dispelled by handshaking all around and other plain manifestations of friendship. The old chief being too weak to walk, presently appeared in a light canoe. He wished to gain as much knowledge as possible of my plans, being especially curious to know why we had come that far, and when we were going to leave. I replied that I had come to ask permission to pass through their grounds for the purpose of looking at the country, and then made general inquiries about the topography of the vicinity. They manifested great fear of us, pretended ignorance of every question, and represented their country as impassable to white men, and the river as deep and swift. As a means of obtaining information, the interview was a failure, but much had been gained by merely bringing about an amicable meeting with these elusive people, who, under most circumstances, would have run away at our approach. Much of their innate suspicion of strangers had been removed, and the display of force proved sufficient to prevent them from molesting any of our men in the future.[1]

[1] In 1875 the Harper's *New Monthly Magazine* published the following, in which there is much poetic license:—

THE SIGN OF THE CROSS

A Narrative Piece.

(Lieutenant Selfridge's Exploring Expedition,
Central America, 1869).

I.

Leaving our ships in the bay,
  We advanced (clearing our pathway day by day)
  Far through the forests and jungles of Central America.

II.

In time ('twas toward night-fall),
    After a long day's journey,
  A day of toil and danger, of hope and forlorn hopes,
We reached a savannah,
And in the distance saw signs of life and of man.

III.

Our coming stirred a group of Indians,
  The ancient red native, wild and naked,
  Who never yet had seen the white man's face,
  Who knew not of his ways or power;
  The white man, whose mysterious apparition
  Raised wonder, if not fear.

IV.

The group advanced to meet us:
With it one who looked the chief, proud though a savage.

V.

As we drew near, he led his side, I mine,
  Each gazing forward with keen inquest,
  To see if the intent were hostile,
  To discern the nature, each of each, the spirit and the purpose.

VI.

He bore his war weapons—spear, and bow and arrows;
  From his head rose feathers;
  Battle-scarred were his face and breast (seen through our glass).
We to him were strange, bearded and white.

VII.

Now, when within due range of visible signal,
  He halted, doubtful, wary,
  Looked toward us, and then, with questioning mien,
He made the SIGN OF THE CROSS.

VIII.

The SIGN OF THE CROSS:
  Raising aloft his warlike spear and bow,
  And crossing his bow upon his spear.

IX.

Discerning quickly his inquiry,
The like sign for reply I gave—
  Crossing two bamboo canes at hand.

X.

Now, hastening forward, he loftily saluted us,
Accepting this high sign
  As proof of friendship, brotherhood, humanity.

XI.

He led us to his tents,
  Where we were feasted on strange game and fruits;
And after being guarded through the night,
On the morrow were sped upon our way.

XII.

This savage chief had never known of Christ,
  The Child of Bethlehem, the Man of Calvary,
  The Son of God who sits at God's right hand;
He knew not of redemption through the Cross,
  Of everlasting life through Christ's heart's blood;
He worshiped unknown gods and Cloud or Sun.

XIII.

But some way,
  From some other age, some tradition,
He had learned the Cross
  Was sign of amity, of peace.
Thus, by THIS SIGN, our lives were saved.

XIV.

And as the Cross revealed new mystic powers,
  Displayed its life to savage as to saint,
To Heaven I raised acclaim:

XV.

O wondrous Cross of Calvary!
  O symbol high and great!
  Eternal Cross! of universal love the sign!
  Man's hope in life, Life's hope beyond the skies!

JOHN SWINTON.

While in the vicinity a pace-traverse was made for several miles beyond the camp, and other scientific data obtained sufficient for our objects. There was no need of going farther inland to determine definitely that Dr. Cullen was quite wrong in his assertions respecting the existence of a low pass in that neighborhood. Our return trip was void of special incident, and we reached the ship on March 3rd after an absence of a week. Having had constant rains we had been wet the entire time, and had encountered the different pests of the jungle, yet not a man returned sick, and all were in fine spirits.

This reconnaissance was followed by others in different localities; meantime the survey work being carried forward simultaneously in several places. From the fact of his having to plan the survey work and to supervise its general progress, the writer found it necessary to accompany nearly all of the exploratory expeditions. The above description of the strenuous nature of the first one is generally applicable to those which were undertaken later. The following extracts from my diary of a trip in April give some further characteristic details:

"Thursday— . . . At half past two o'clock we forded the LaPaz; this was the deepest river we had met, the water coming up to our arm pits, and obliging us to carry our ammunition and provisions on our heads. Several Bungo trees full of monkeys were seen, as many as 20 or 30 in a tree; some were shot and proved a pleasant and much needed repast. . . .

"Friday—Broke camp at half past six o'clock. Eugenio, a machetero, was bitten during the night by a scorpion or tarantula, and his leg and foot became so swelled that we were forced to leave him behind. At 4 o'clock went into camp. Passed a miserable night tormented by mosquitoes and sand flies.

"Saturday—Started down the right bank of the river. Left behind nine men who were shoeless. Cut through 5,000 feet, a dense grove of mangrove; found footprints of Indians all along the river bank. At noon, while crossing the river, our barometer was broken. After dinner, in consequence of this accident and our provisions running low, we took up our return march. . . .

"Sunday—Another sleepless night on account of insects. A number of men were shoeless; cut up shelter tents, haversacks, etc., to supply the need. At 7 o'clock started on our march, and at 10 o'clock came up with the machetero Eugenio, who was sufficiently recovered to keep up with the rear guard. . . . at 5 o'clock went into camp; the provisions running low, the men were allowed to collect wild plantains. Henceforth our meals consisted of plantains, bacon, and coffee, the bread being about all gone.

"Monday—Broke camp at half past six. At the junction of the Chucanaqua and Sucubti met two Asnati Indians, and asked them to guide me, but they declined, saying a few miles farther on we should meet some of the Sucubtis. After wandering a long time, losing our way, we arrived at camp No. 2. Here we found the wounded Marine (accidentally shot on the preceding Thursday and left behind) and his attendant, whom the Indians had treated with respect, giving them provisions, but had told them that if we did not return that night they would have to leave in the morning. At half past one, no Indians having appeared, we continued up the river, but shortly met four canoe loads of them. They shook hands all around and intimated we were to follow them. Soon two others were met; these we followed by a very good trail, through a beautiful country, passing plantations and villages. At half past four went into camp. While collecting grass for a bed, one of the macheta-men was bitten by a tarantula.

"Tuesday—Called all hands at early daylight. . . . (The guides) showed a vast deal more alacrity in showing us out of their country than the way through it, the trail the whole way on our return being very easy walking. . . . By noon we were at camp No. 1, our first stopping place. While passing through their villages not a woman was seen; and in houses apparently deserted, on looking back, 20 or 30 Indians could be seen, showing how completely they could conceal themselves in the jungle. . . . Went into camp at five o'clock. Had a very scanty supper of wild plantains and coffee.

"Wednesday—Broke camp at the usual hour; had to go without breakfast, as we consumed the last of our provisions the evening before. At ten o'clock everyone had reached our main camp on the Sucubti, and ate the first hearty meal we had had for three days. . . . Reached the beach in the afternoon. Nearly all were shoeless and worn out, but most everyone in good health."

The successful accomplishment of this reconnaissance moved me to publish the following order:

"UNITED STATES STEAMER NIPSIC,
"April 13, 1870.
"To the officers, seamen, and marines
composing surveying-party No. 1:
"Upon your return from the arduous duties of the past two months, your commanding officer

deems it a proper moment to congratulate you upon the success you have achieved. You have opened to the world an almost unknown wilderness; you have procured information that others before you have sought for and failed.

"That this has not been done without great sacrifice on your part, your commander is well aware; but he has watched with pride the patience with which you have endured want and hardship, the perseverance with which you have overcome the obstacles that surrounded you, and the zeal with which you have seconded his wishes in promoting the objects of the expedition.

"Still greater efforts he may require of you, but he knows you will meet them in the same spirit as you have overcome the past, and upon your return to your homes you will all remember with pride the part you have borne in the expedition of 1870.

"Thos. O. Selfridge,

"Commander, commanding Darien Expedition."

By the middle of April sufficient data had been collected and recorded to demonstrate the impracticability of a low level ship canal through the hills back of Caledonia Bay, except by a long and very costly tunnel. Accordingly the theatre of operations was moved to the Gulf of San Blas. Here also was an excellent harbor, to serve as the Atlantic terminus for a possible canal, across the shortest transit to be found anywhere on the

Isthmus. Directly opposite, the large Chepo River emptied into the Pacific, and some of its branches had their headwaters in mountains close to the Gulf of San Blas. The height of the lowest depressions through these mountains would settle the question of the practicability of this route. On our arrival at San Blas the period of heavy rains was at hand, but I was anxious to collect sufficient data either to condemn this line or to indicate the wisdom of a further survey next season. In the distance a deep cut in the mountain range could be seen from the anchorage, which led to the hope that the long wished for route might be found here. The well known absence of Indians in the interior of this country promised to enable the work to proceed with greater despatch than previously had been possible.

But the swampy nature of the coast country, combined with heavy rains, proved greater obstacles than unfriendly Indians. We managed to locate the mouth of the principal river, and to cut a boat passage through heavy mangroves, before the worst rains began. After that, many delays were caused by the river overflowing its banks and flooding the extensive lowlands. Often the current was so strong as to sweep boats down stream in spite of their oars. Yet within a month we reached the gap in the mountains. Here the altitude of 300 feet was disappointing and prophetic; but in order to decide definitely upon the practicability of this route, it was necessary to carry our levels over the isthmian divide which lay beyond, and if this could be done that year it would obviate the necessity of a return to the vicinity next season.

The stock of provisions in the ships was nearly exhausted; the crews were worn out by fatigue and no longer inspired by the novelty of the work; the macheteros were discontented at being kept beyond the term of their agreement; our supply of shoes was so low as to make it difficult to equip a dozen men, and the rains threatened to burst upon us at any moment, rendering the return of the field parties exceedingly difficult and dangerous. Yet I was loath to abandon the work in such a stage as would require its resumption the following year. On May 23rd, two officers upon whose pluck and energy I could rely, Lieutenants Hitchcock and Goodrell, were ordered to select volunteers and carry the survey as far over the divide as their provisions would permit. The top of the ridge was crossed on June 7th, at an altitude of 1,142 feet, and the survey continued for several miles on the Pacific slope. We had gathered all the necessary data to prove the line impracticable, with the engineering facilities of that period, owing to the excessive length of tunneling required for a low level canal. Our laborious season was soon afterwards terminated by departing for the United States, where, to the never failing inner reward incident to the successful accomplishment of every difficult task, was added the following from the Secretary of the Navy:

"Washington, July 7, 1870,
"Navy Department.

"Sir: I congratulate you upon your return from the preliminary survey of the Isthmus of Darien.

"I take this opportunity to state to you how much gratified I feel at the efficient and energetic manner in which you and your officers and men, and the civilians who were associated with you, have carried out the wishes and instructions of the Department.

"I beg leave to say to you that you have fully met my expectations in the amount of work performed; and although you have not been able as yet to find a practicable route for a ship-canal, you have gained a large amount of very valuable information, which will be useful to science, give the world geographical knowledge hitherto unknown, and settle all doubts regarding a communication between the Atlantic and Pacific Oceans at those points already surveyed.

"I desire you will express to all those under your command my appreciation of their zeal and enterprise under very trying circumstances.

"I remain, very respectfully, your obedient servant,

"Geo. M. Robeson,
"Secretary of the Navy.
"Commander Thomas O. Selfridge,
"United States Navy, Washington, D. C."

Following is a list of officers and civilians attached to the expedition of 1870 for the survey of the Isthmus of Darien.

OFFICERS

UNITED STATES STEAMER NIPSIC

Commander Thomas O. Selfridge, Commanding.
Lieutenant S. Hubbard.
Lieutenant E. McCormack.
Master G. S. Davol.
Ensign J. S. Moser.
Ensign R. T. Jasper.
Ensign N. E. Niles.

Passed Assistant Paymaster J. P. Loomis.
Passed Assistant Surgeon W. J. Simon.
First Assistant Engineer W. S. Smith.
Second Assistant Engineer L. C. Safford.

Captain's clerk, E. G. Casey.

UNITED STATES SHIP GUARD

Commander E. P. Lull.
Lieutenant G. S. Schulze.
Lieutenant R. D. Hitchcock.
Master F. Collins.
Master J. G. Eaton.
Ensign A. Elliot.
Ensign J. M. Hawley.

Passed Assistant Paymaster F. Bissell.
Assistant Surgeon A. Griffith.
Captain of marines, G. P. Houston.
Lieutenant of marines, M. G. Goodrell.

Lieutenant of marines, S. K. Allen.

CIVILIANS

Assistant J. A. Sullivan, U. S. Coast Survey.
Assistant A. T. Mossman, U. S. Coast Survey.
Sub-Assistant H. G. Ogden, U. S. Coast Survey.
Sub-Assistant H. L. Merinden, U. S. Coast Survey.
Draughtsman L. Karcher, U. S. Coast Survey.

Mineralogist, J. P. Carson.
Mineralogist, E. W. Bowditch.
Chief Telegrapher, W. H. Clarke.
Assistant Telegrapher, Calvin McDowell.
Assistant Telegrapher, A. J. Gustin. (Discharged for misconduct at Cartagena, South America.)

Photographer, T. H. O'Sullivan.

CHAPTER XVIII

A CASUAL examination of the map opposite page 161, will disclose the basic conditions underlying the second season's work on the Isthmus of Darien. As described in the preceding chapter, the two canal routes beginning on the Atlantic side at the Gulf of San Blas and Caledonia Bay, had been definitely eliminated by the high land existing in the immediate vicinity of those harbors.

The only other possible Atlantic origin of a canal was from the vicinity of the Gulf of Darien, which terminates at its south end in a splendid harbor, which we named Columbus Bay. Here is the delta of the Atrato River, a magnificent stream, navigable for deep-draft vessels from the easily dredged delta bars through a distance of about two hundred miles inland. From the generally north and south axis of the Atrato, a number of large tributaries branch toward the Pacific Ocean. The first of these has its headwaters in mountains near mid-Isthmus, only a few miles across a divide from streams on the Pacific slope, which feed the great bay of San Miguel. Previous reports of several explorers had stated this dividing ridge to be less than 200 feet in height, thus encouraging the belief that here lay a very promising line for our survey.

Farther to the south several other large tributaries of the Atrato rose in mountains only a few miles distant from the Pacific Ocean. The headwaters of one of these was opposite Humboldt Bay, but the possibility of a route in that locality had been eliminated by the joint Army and Navy survey conducted in 1857-58 by Michler and Craven. Another of these large tributaries called the Napipi River, had its source within the very short distance of three miles from the excellent anchorage of Cupica Bay, on the Pacific coast. A negro whom I met at Aspinwall first called my attention to this route, by stating that in a few hours' walk over a comparatively low and easy trail, he traversed the distance between the Pacific Ocean and the Napipi River. The proper exploration of the only two possible routes mentioned above required operations from both the Atlantic and the Pacific sides, and arrangements were accordingly made for the services of a vessel from the Pacific Fleet to cooperate with the *Nipsic* and the *Guard.*

The writer sailed from New York in the *Guard,* in advance of the *Nipsic,* on December 3, 1870, and after fourteen days reached Cartagena where sixteen natives were procured, together with a well-recommended guide. Columbia Bay was reached on December 27th, and a hydrographic survey of that vicinity including the river delta, was immediately begun by Commander Lull, assisted by Lieutenant Hawley. Plans for the work inland required a preliminary reconnaissance, and on January 2nd I started up the Atrato River, accompanied by Lieutenant Couden, five sailors, two marines, and two natives, including the guide, in a steam launch towing a flat boat containing twelve days' rations. We had had two of these flat boats constructed in New York in anticipation of having to survey through swampy ground. They were 24 ft. by 5 ft., and drew only ten inches of water when carrying ten men with twelve days' provsions, and proved exceedingly useful.

A short passage through one of the delta mouths brought us to the main river, and we were amazed to find it many hundred yards wide, in some places one hundred feet deep, and with long reaches as far as the eye could see. Its low banks, covered with a dense tropical growth, were submerged by the floods for a depth of about two feet during nine months of the year. At sunset we anchored near the mouth of the Cacarica River, the branch mentioned above, which rises in the transverse mid-isthmus watershed. After a night of torment from dense swarms of mosquitoes, we passed into the Cacarica, whose mouth was thirty feet deep and wide enough for ship navigation. Progress of the steam launch was soon seriously interrupted by grammatote-grass, which covers most of the surface of this river and is so strong and thick that the wake of a boat pushed through it will hardly show any water.

Leaving the steam launch behind with orders to await my return, I took the flat boat with Mr. Couden, the guide Remedio, and eight sailors, and proceeded up river. Exhausting labor on the part of all hands was required to push the boat through the heavy growth of grass with the oars. Our thirst became intolerable, since we had neglected to fill the canteens from the river below and were afraid to drink the stagnant waters of the swamp. About 4 P.M. we got out of the grass and entered a swampy country, covered with a dense growth of palms, through which ran a narrow and shallow channel, so tortuous that we never could have found our way but for the skill of the guide. At sunset we cooked supper by a fire built upon the roots of a palm tree, and then spent the night in the boat tormented by myriads of mosquitoes. The next morning the inside of the awning was black with them.

The whole of the following day, January 4th, was passed in this dark and slimy swamp, the overgrowth being so thick as rarely to permit a glimpse of the sun, and the path so narrow and the water so shoal, as frequently to compel us to hew away the obstructions or to wade through the mire, pushing the boat ahead. Every leaf seemed to hold a family of ants, which sometimes came down in showers when the boat touched a limb, and their sharp bites were almost as annoying as the mosquitoes. That night we stopped at a miry strip of ground about six inches above water, and the only rest obtainable was through rolling up in blankets, and snatching little naps in this smothered state.

The next day was very similar. Desperate from want of sleep, we worked with a will, hoping to reach high ground to escape from our winged persecutors, who seemed to be the only inhabitants of this dark and dismal swamp, except jaguars whose distant growls could be heard occasionally. At about three o'clock we emerged from the oppressive jungle into the open river, but the current became so swift as greatly to retard our progress. Heavy rains that day continued through the night, and made the current so strong by the following morning that Remedio declared it impossible to push our laden boat up stream. However, in spite of the five-knot current, I determined to keep going, since our provisions had already been heavily depleted, and we had not covered a third of the journey. With the assistance of a lead-line, the boat was tracked up stream by hauling from the bank; but this was laborious work, as heavy cutting was required through a thick growth of wild plantains and vines before the line could be carried ahead. At one place an immense drift pile necessitated taking everything out of the boat and hauling her bodily overland to the river above. In another similar place, where the trees would not permit a land portage, two hours were spent in clearing a passage through the drift. We made only about two miles during the whole day's work, but it was a distinct gain finally to clear the swamp and see the sky above. That evening the luxury was afforded of leaving the cramped quarters of the boat and camping on banks two feet out of water. At midnight however the banks overflowed, after a heavy downpour, driving all hands into the boat, where a sleepless night was passed.

The next morning, January 7th, it was still raining hard. Everybody was soaking wet, cold, and uncomfortable. The water was two feet deep over what had been dry ground the previous day, and the Cacarica had become a foaming torrent, making it impossible to proceed. There being no place to build a fire, we were obliged to breakfast on raw bacon and hard bread. At noon the rain stopped, the sun came out, and soon all hands, wading knee-deep, were busily engaged in drying their clothes upon the trees and bushes. The river was too swift to permit moving until the following morning, when we proceeded tediously against the strong current at a rate of about one mile an hour, delayed occasionally by small rapids. The depletion of our provisions required putting everyone on half rations.

On January 9th, the adverse current still forbade any progress under oars, and the boat had to be poled. Finally the river became a series of rapids, requiring all hands to go overboard and push or pull the boat, the torrent frequently sweeping us off our feet. By 5 P. M. a point had been reached, beyond which the river was reported practically impassable, and I decided to make the rest of the journey on foot.

In the morning, leaving one man in charge of the boat, we took the trail for the village of Paya, carrying knapsacks, blankets, rifles, and four days' provisions. It was necessary to wade the river through most of the tedious day. From 7 P.M. the rain came down in torrents and soon put out our fire. There was no choice but to sit out the long pitchy black night with blankets over our heads, to keep off the mosquitoes, which seemed more vindictive than ever. By universal choice this stopping place was dubbed "Camp Misery."

At 2 P.M. the next day we stood on the crest of the divide, at a height of about 170 feet above the plain of the river at the point we had left it. The principal object had been attained in reaching the highest point of our survey of this route, and so low was the altitude that hopes ran high of having discovered the long sought canal route; especially since reports on the Pacific slope of the ridge, made by other explorers, had been very favorable. The climb had been so exhausting that, notwithstanding the early hour, camp was made on the ridge.

Shortly after the following noon we reached the village of Paya, whose inhabitants I desired to propitiate. Some presents had been brought, including a gold-headed tortoise shell cane, a double-barrelled shotgun, and pieces of bright cotton prints, and their distribution resulted in such amicable relations that we were provided with chickens, eggs, and a night's lodgings. The Indians, however, with their usual hypocrisy and cunning, contended that the path by which we had crossed was the only one known to them.

I had intended to return that afternoon, but the guide Remedio had been imbibing freely and absolutely refused to go. We left the next morning, the 13th, having considerable trouble in making the guide accompany us, as he was still very drunk. One of the men of the party was so footsore that he had to be left behind; arrangements being made with the chief to send him down the Tuyra River, on the Pacific slope, to Pinogana Bay, whence he could find transport to Panama.

Noon of the 14th found us at the Cacarica, where we met a portion of the surveying party which had been left behind at its mouth. They had followed us up, but a shortage of provisions had persuaded them to proceed to Paya, contrary to my instructions to base on the camp at the mouth of the Cacarica. The meeting was fortunate, because without a guide they would never have found the village; on the other hand, the little store of provisions which the reconnoitering party had carefully husbanded, had now to be divided, and only a scanty amount could be allotted to each man. Two days later we reached the steam launch at the mouth of the Cacarica, and on the following day, January 17th, arrived at the ship after an absence of sixteen days. The hardships of this reconnaissance brought many of the party down with fever, myself included. The guide, Remedio, was seized with brain fever and died after an illness of three days.

The *Nipsic* arrived at Columbia Bay on January 30th, and on February 8th I embarked on her for Aspinwall, with the intention of exploring the Pacific side of the Isthmus; leaving the *Guard* behind to continue surveys of Columbia harbor, and of the prospective canal route across the divide in the vicinity of Paya. On February 14th, after having crossed the Isthmus by rail and joined the *Resaca,* my party reached the Gulf of San Miguel which, as has been previously explained, is the outlet for the Tuyra River, whose headwaters lie in the same mid-isthmian ridge that I had just explored from the Atlantic approaches. It was also necessary to explore and survey the Pacific side before the practicability of this route could be decided.

Immediately after anchoring at the head of ship navigation on the Tuyra, about 30 miles from the sea, work was begun with a view to connecting up with the parties operating from the Atlantic side. Two reconnaissances by the writer gave him sufficient information of the river, to a point within 30 miles of the dividing ridge, to enable him to put several survey parties in the field and lay out a general plan for their guidance. Then, with the ship, he proceeded farther south along the coast to Cupica Bay, the harbor previously mentioned as being close to the headwaters of the Napipi River, a large branch of the great Atrato on the Atlantic watershed.

Local information at Cupica corroborated the reports of the lowness of the narrow divide between the Pacific Ocean and the Napipi headwaters, but exploration of that river could be readily undertaken only in canoes, which were not available nearer than the Atrato River. They were sent for by native messenger, and meantime a survey of the Pacific side of the gap was begun. The trail led up through a beautiful gorge of the small Limon River, which at one point has a precipitate fall of 250 feet. Without great difficulty the low point of the ridge was determined to be 612 feet above sea level. While this height was too great for a surface canal, the narrowness of the ridge suggested the possibility of tunneling through it. The crest of the ridge is rarely over 12 feet wide, and in some places not more than 5 feet, and so steep that towards the Pacific one can look almost directly upon the tops of the trees beneath.

In the vicinity of Cupica Bay I had two unusual experiences with wild animals. One afternoon while walking along a trail through the jungle, a jaguar appeared from the underbrush directly in front of me, and only about twenty yards distant. There it crouched and glared at me. Being alone and having no other weapon than a walking stick, naturally I stopped precipitately, and hastily considered what course was best to take. Reasoning that to run would encourage pursuit and attack, I merely stood still and returned the steady stare. Finally the jaguar slunk off into the jungle and disappeared.

On another afternoon I went ashore for a swim, in a beautiful pool near the mouth of the Limon River. After undressing I jumped in feet first, and landed on something soft near the bottom. To my complete surprise a great commotion and splashing began immediately, quite sufficient to cause my instant race for the bank. There safety was reached just in time to see a large alligator, emerging in equal haste from the opposite side of the pool. I believe that the author is the only naval officer who can justly claim to have ridden an alligator!

Twelve days after our arrival word came that the canoes from the Atrato had at last reached the head of canoe navigation on the Napipi, and the next morning I left the ship with my steward and four other men, with eight days' provisions. In an hour and a half we had crossed the divide and reached the source of the Napipi, and five hours later had found the canoes, twelve miles from the ocean. All the way the trail had been wide and clear, with many nearly level stretches.

In the morning I embarked in the smallest canoe, with two natives, and pushed on ahead, leaving the rest of the party with the two larger canoes, to proceed more slowly while surveying. A day and a half later, with little difficulty, I reached the Atrato, and was so greatly impressed by its grandeur, half a mile wide and 30 feet deep even at that distance from the Atlantic, that a note was despatched to Commander Lull, by a passing barquetona bound to Cartagena, instructing him to make a survey of the Atrato, from the Napipi to its mouth. The night was spent near a fisherman's hut.

Next morning, the return journey was begun, and while progress against the current was of course slower, no great difficulties were encountered. Hard rains seemed to bring all bird life to the river. Numerous flocks of wild turkeys, and at least twenty different species of brilliantly colored birds were observed. The whole round trip, from the ocean to the mouth of the Atrato and return, was completed in a little more than seven days. This reconnaissance had developed much more favorable results than I could have hoped for. The subsequent surveys showed a route only thirty-one miles long, between the Pacific Ocean and the navigable Atrato, twenty miles of this distance being a nearly level plain.

Leaving survey parties behind, the *Resaca* returned to Panama for stores, and thence hastened to San Miguel Bay to reprovision the parties left on the Tuyra. These latter had caused me much anxiety, from having been abandoned to their own resources for such a long time, but happily the intelligence of them was good. After replenishing their base with supplies, the ship proceeded to Cupica Bay, picked up the Napipi parties, and again returned to the Tuyra River, where concentrated efforts were necessary if the work was to be finished before the height of the rainy season.

It was fortunate that, anticipating the possibility of undue delays, the general plan for surveying the Tuyra region had required completion of the remote hill district, near the trans-isthmian divide, before beginning the comparatively easy section of the lower river. Contrary to the impression given by a view of the upper river from nearby heights, the survey parties encountered very rough country on both sides of the stream. This circumstance delayed the finish of the more inland section until

May 15th, a date that I had counted upon for the completion of the whole work in the Pacific. We were then in the midst of the rainy season, which not only increased the labor of the survey work, and the proneness to sickness, but also made it nearly impossible to send provisions up the Tuyra, whose current sometimes reached a velocity of five knots. Moreover we were embarrassed further by the refusal of our native men to work any more, on the plea that the contracted period of their employment had expired.

On May 17th, after several days of heavy rains, the river overflowed and threatened to stop further operations of the field parties, which had then reached the low country. A detail of this eventful night is supplied from the log of the officer in charge ashore.

"At 11.30 P. M., river rose over the banks and flooded the camp. Took candles and started back in hopes of reaching high ground. Waded neck deep, candles went out, and was glad to get back. Secured instruments and provisions in trees. At midnight, water being two feet deep in camp and rising, took to the trees ourselves. Water continued to rise until 4 A. M., when the camp was from 4 to 7 feet under water. Flood commenced to subside very slowly at 4.30 A. M. Total rise of water above high water, 15 feet. All hands perched in trees all night, from which we came down at 7 o'clock, waist deep in water, and managed, after some difficulty, in making a fire upon a raft, to cook some coffee. As the river was falling very slowly, gave the order to construct rafts and return to Pinogana. Left the camp at 10 A.M. on a raft, and arrived in 4½ hours. These rafts were constructed of the bolsa tree, a wood as light as cork."

This discouraging misfortune led me to assume charge of the field operations in person, with fresh men from the ship to replace the sick. The line led over low but steep hills, and slippery mud made walking very fatiguing. Five days of exceedingly hard work, during which several of the men had to be sent back to the ship from sickness or exhaustion, finally finished the line. This survey party under Lieutenant Eaton had made an extraordinary record. They had been absent from the ship one hundred days, and had run a line of levels fifty-eight miles, through dense forests, and over precipitous hills, deep ravines, and almost impassable swamps.

The *Resaca* sailed for Panama on June 3rd, to await the arrival of the *Guard* at Aspinwall from the Gulf of Darien. The Atlantic division of the expedition, under the able direction of Commander Lull, prosecuted their work with skill and vigor during my absence in the Pacific. In spite of the extraordinary obstacles which my reconnaissance of the Cacarica had disclosed, the region was surveyed up to the trans-isthmian ridge, and a further survey carried along the ridge to ascertain its lowest point. The great Atrato River, from the sea to the mouth of the Napipi, and the extensive Columbia Bay were also surveyed. A reconnaissance was also made of the so-called DePuydt route, to investigate reports made by a Frenchman of that name, that in 1865 he had discovered a passage across the isthmus not exceeding 150 feet in height, in the region of the Tanela River, to the south of the Atrato.

This reconnaissance was made by Lieutenant Commander Schulze, who ascended the Tanela River some 33 miles. At the forks he was met by a large body of Indians, who refused him permission to go any farther. After hours of parleying, in which he warned the Indians that a refusal to let him pass would surely result in the return of a great American Chief with a large force which would pass without permission, the party was allowed to continue. An elevation of 638 feet was reached, with higher mountains visible several miles farther inland, and with this proof of the falsity of DePuydt's information the party returned to the ship.

Three weeks after the Pacific division reached Panama in the *Resaca,* the *Guard* arrived at Aspinwall, the *Nipsic* being detained to verify the position of certain headlands in the Gulf of Darien.

The Pacific division was at once transferred across the Isthmus, and the *Guard* sailed for home on June 30th.

Following is a list of the officers and civilians attached to the Darien exploring expedition of 1871.

OFFICERS

Commander Thomas O. Selfridge, commanding expedition.

Commander E. P. Lull, commanding United States ship *Guard*.

Lieutenant Commander G. C. Schulze.

Master J. P. Merrell.

Master A. R. Couden.

Master J. T. Sullivan.

Master A. Elliot.

Master J. M. Hawley.

Passed Assistant Paymaster Frank Bissell.

Assistant Surgeon H. C. Eckstein.

Second Assistant Engineer J. W. Hollihan.

Midshipman R. G. Peck.

Midshipman C. P. Kunhardt.

Midshipman J. J. Hunker.

Midshipman T. G. C. Salter.

Midshipman J. H. Bull.

Lieutenant George A. Norris.

Master Fred Collins.

Master J. G. Eaton.

Ensign E. H. Wiley.

Ensign S. C. Paine.

Ensign B. H. Buckingham.

Acting Passed Assistant Surgeon Linneus Fussell.

CIVILIANS

James Barnes, civil engineer.

A. Leslie Duvall, civil engineer.

A. D. Beach, civil engineer.

G. A. Maacke, geologist.

F. Blake, Coast Survey astronomer.

John Moran, photographer.

A. Pohlers, draughtsman.

CHAPTER XIX

AFTER arrival in the United States, an analysis of the great mass of data which had been collected during the second year of survey revealed two outstanding facts. The route over the mid-isthmus divide, between the headwaters of the Tuyra and the Cacarica, seemed impracticable by reason of the enormous amount of excavation required. The Napipi route was regarded very favorably, upon the assumption that a ship tunnel was feasible, and my own affirmative belief in the matter was confirmed by the opinions of a number of eminent engineers whom I consulted. Among these was B. H. Latrobe, Esq., of the Baltimore and Ohio Railroad, J. B. Francis, Esq., of Lowell, Mr. J. Dutton Steele, and Mr. Walter Shanley, the successful engineer and contractor of the Hoosac tunnel. The latter wrote:

"The section you showed me presents a much less impracticable route than from all I had learned of those previously explored, I imagined could be obtained. A tunnel of the dimensions you contemplate is not all tunnel, in the tunneler's sense of the term; that is to say the work would not all have to be done by the expensive process incident to boring. First, drive a tunnel properly such, say 10 or 15 feet high at the top, and all the rest could and should be treated as "open cut," and as such need not cost more per cubic yard than a cubic yard of similar rock on other parts of the work."

This opinion related to a proposed tunnel about six miles in length. The next season's work was to find a route where only about three miles of tunneling would be required. Considering the extraordinary advances that have been made in engineering practice—power drills, explosives, dredgers, reinforced concrete (eliminating masonry work), etc.—since 1872, when the above expert opinions were expressed there seems little doubt that today a tunnel could be readily cut, not only in the Napipi region, but also through the necessary twelve miles at San Blas. The latter route has the advantages over any other, of the least distance across the Isthmus and a splendid harbor at each end.

The work of the expedition of 1873 was to ascertain whether better access existed from the Pacific to the Atrato River by way of any of the tributaries lying south of the Napipi. The region to be explored, being confined in extent, did not require so large an expedition as in the two previous years.

In January, Lieutenants Collins, Eaton, and Sullivan, Assistant Paymaster Ring, and the writer, proceeded by passenger steamer to Aspinwall, and joined the *Tuscarora* (Commander Belknap) at Panama. In a few days survey parties had been landed at Limon Bay, and Chiri-Chiri Bay, seven miles farther south. The latter place was near the headwaters of the Bojaya, a large tributary of the Atrato.

While the two survey parties were at work, the writer, in company with Lieutenant Collins, a sailor as interpreter, and two canoe men, made a reconnaissance of three hundred miles to the Atrato River and return, exploring the Bojaya and its principal tributary, the Cuia, as well as the upper reaches of the Atrato itself. While of course many hardships were encountered, they were less severe than those previously described as incident to other trips. One morning, about a mile below Quibo, on the upper Atrato, we passed a large number of women washing for gold, on a partially dry bar in the middle of the river. We learned it was considered a good day's work to make a dollar in this way. All the tributaries flowing into the right bank of the upper Atrato are gold bearing. The deposit of the precious metal in these mountains must be immense, but it is extremely difficult to gain any information from the natives as to the location of gold. I once asked an intelligent Indian living on the Doguado River if there was gold in the mountains; pointing up river he replied, "Yes." Promises to make him rich if he would show me the deposits only resulted in a negative head shake and a protest that his people would kill him. The tradition of misfortune in connection with gold, handed down from the ancestors of these people, has instilled a universal and unshakable resolution never to reveal the existence of gold to a white man.

The result of my reconnaissance proved conclusively that this route was inferior to the Napipi. There remained now nothing to be explored but the valley of the Doguado, a southerly tributary of the Napipi. The day after our return both Mr. Collins and myself were attacked with severe fever, which kept us so weak as to prevent further work on shore. The exploration of the Doguado was therefore entrusted to Ensign Taut, assisted by Midshipman Galt, and their efforts, combined with those of the survey parties already mentioned, disclosed what is undoubtedly the best canal route in this vicinity. In my final reports to the Department this line was recommended in preference to any others discovered during the whole of the three years' work on the Isthmus.

The proposed route embraced a part of the survey of the previous year; from Columbia Bay on the Atlantic side, up the Atrato River to the Napipi, and thence paralleled that tributary to a point near the mouth of the Doguado. From this point the route branched into the valley of the Doguado to the isthmian divide, through which it passed by tunnel to the headwaters of the Chiri-Chiri River, and thence down the valley of that river to the Pacific Ocean. The navigability of the Atrato rendered it necessary to canalize only the short distance of twenty-eight miles, from the point where the route leaves that river to the Pacific. The level plain along the lower Napipi, and the lower Doguado, reduced the necessary excavation to moderate proportions, and the length of tunnel required under the divide was only three miles. The valley of the Chiri-Chiri River lent itself to the installation of a series of locks, needed to make the descent from the tunnel mouth to the ocean, and Chiri-Chiri Bay was capable of development into a suitable harbor by the construction of a break-water; a work that could be relatively cheaply done by dumping rock from the tunnel excavation.

The discovery of this, the only practicable route for a canal that it was possible to construct with the engineering facilities of that period, was a triumph for the expedition. In addition we had gathered comprehensive data of every possible route across Darien, to serve the purposes of prob-able future progress in engineering science. All this had been accomplished in spite of the almost insuperable difficulties interposed by nature, which for centuries had prevented others from achieving similar results.

Too much credit cannot be given to my splendid subordinates for their efficiency, resourcefulness, and resolution, under long continued and extremely trying conditions. Lieutenants Collins, Eaton, and Sullivan volunteered to accompany me on the final expedition notwithstanding an intimate knowledge, gained from preceding years, of the hardships to be endured. The two former participated in the work of all three seasons. Commander Lull shared with me much of the responsibility of the operations. It will be recalled that while I was at work on the Pacific side during the second season, he was in charge of a larger force on the Atlantic watershed. During the two most difficult first years his assistance proved almost indispensable. Others who engaged in the strenuous labors of two successive seasons were Lieutenant-Commander Schulze and Masters Elliot and Hawley. These younger officers, together with a number of others whose names appear in my published official report (Government Printing Office, 1874), often spent weeks at a time in remote parts of the jungle, exposed to all the dangers from Indians, climate, insects, and animals, yet successfully carried on precise survey work in spite of extremely great hardships. I cannot adequately express the gratitude and admiration I feel towards them all.

*   *   *   *   *

My final reports on the Darien surveys were scarcely completed before Secretary Robeson sent me to Toronto to inspect the records of the Confederate State Department, which had been offered for sale to our government by a Mr. Pickett. During the chaotic days immediately after the fall of Richmond in 1864, these documents had been surreptitiously removed to Canada by him and a few other accomplices. My examination disclosed a large and highly interesting collection, containing not only naval and military records, but also state papers, all the letters of Slidell and Mason to Benjamin, the Secretary of State, and at my suggestion the purchase was made for $30,000. Among these papers was a letter from a rebel spy named Kennedy, containing a plan of setting fire to Northern hotels and placing bombs in the coal bunkers of steamers. It was an atrocious document, and its publication was sufficient to brand the author as a rascal, and to exert a considerable influence upon the course of the presidential campaign, in favor of Grant's election.

For three years (1872-75) I served as Aide to the Commandant of the Boston Navy Yard, and after this duty had been completed, the Department granted me eighteen months' leave, which was spent in Utah managing a mining company, owned principally by a group of my Boston friends. My headquarters were in Salt Lake City, where I occupied a house belonging to Ann Eliza, a wife of Brigham Young—the nineteenth in point of seniority—who had gone east following a marital difference with her multiply-blessed husband.

My venture in business was attended by reasonable success, but this never tempted me to give up my profession, and at the expiration of the long leave an opportunity to return to a greater salt lake was welcomed. The Commanding officer of the *Enterprise* had asked to be relieved, feeling himself not sufficiently experienced to conduct a survey of the Amazon River, to which duty the ship had been assigned. On account of my previous service at Darien the Department called me to Washington and asked me to undertake the work. This appealed to my professional pride and I was glad to volunteer.

The proposed survey was incident to an effort then being made to open up Bolivia and the vast territory of south central Brazil to communication with the outside world. The fact that all the tributaries entering the Amazon from the south are blocked by extensive rapids, had always been a great detriment to the development of this rich region. The principal one of these tributaries, the Madeira River, was known to be navigable both below and above a series of rapids, which extend for 250 miles. In 1868 the concession of a railroad or canal around these rapids of the Madeira had been granted to a company organized by George E. Church, Esq., of New York. After several abortive attempts had been made to build a railroad, a contract for its construction was let in 1878 to Collins & Company of Philadelphia. This firm encountered great difficulty in transporting material, supplies, and workmen from Para, at the mouth of the Amazon, and requested our government to survey the Madeira River to determine its navigability for steamers of considerable size. It was in response to this request that the *Enterprise* was being sent.

Compared with the Isthmus survey, that of the Madeira and Amazon was mere child's play. But few preparations were required. Permission had to be obtained to enter the Madeira River, since the opening of the Amazon to the ships of all nations in 1867 had not included its tributaries. The State Department promised to obtain the necessary permit from the Brazilian government, and have it awaiting the *Enterprise* on her arrival at Para. The ship itself could supply most of the needed instruments and materials, as well as personnel. A few additional supplies were ordered for her, and the services of a Mr. Sparrow, C. E., who had had previous experience in surveys of the upper Amazon, were obtained. It was necessary to have two officers expert in navigation, since positions at intervals of about twenty-five miles along the river banks had to be determined very accurately by stellar observations. The Executive Officer of the *Enterprise,* Lieutenant S. H. Baker, was thoroughly competent to act as one of these observers, and for the other the Department agreed to send me Lieutenant C. P. Perkins.

These arrangements complete, I left Washington to join the ship at Norfolk, via steamer taken at Baltimore. On boarding the latter Lieutenant Hamilton Perkins, an old friend, was accosted with "Hello, Perkins, what are you doing here?" He answered with obviously feigned cheerfulness, "I am on my way to report to you for duty on the *Enterprise.*" Knowing that the duty upon which the *Enterprise* had been assigned was not attractive, and realizing that a mistake had been made at the Department in detailing the wrong Lieutenant Perkins, I thought to have a little fun at his expense, by temporarily keeping secret the fact of the mistake. That evening he could disguise his depression but poorly, while relating at length how his sudden orders had deprived him from making an interesting trip with a friend and his daughter in a private car. The next morning, on my exposing my perfidy, he tried rather to take backwater by saying, "Captain, I really would have liked to go with you except for the chance of my excursion." A telegram to the Department served to correct the mistake, and not long afterwards my traveling companion married the daughter. Then I was better able to sympathize with his depression over the prospect of several months in remote Brazil.

CHAPTER XX

THE AMAZON EXPEDITION

A DETAILED account of the survey of the Madeira
and Amazon Rivers by the *Enterprise* is contained
in the Report of the Secretary of the Navy to the
President for the year 1879, and therefore need not
be repeated at length herein.

We sailed from Norfolk on May 2d, 1878, and
arrived at the Amazon Delta three weeks later.
Calls upon the Governor of the Province, at Para,
and the American Consul, failed to reveal any
trace of the permit to enter the Madeira River.
Since time pressed this was embarrassing, but feeling confident that our State Department would
obtain the necessary authorization, I concluded not
to wait at Para beyond May 30th, but to proceed
to the mouth of the Madeira where, by that time,
there seemed a reasonable assurance of the permit
reaching me.

Four days were spent steaming through the
narrow passages of the delta, anchoring at night.
Nothing of the size and draft of the *Enterprise* had

ever been up the Amazon, so that too much trust could not be placed in the pilots we had taken, and the lead had to be depended upon, especially in making landings. On the first day we grounded once, but backed off without difficulty. The second night's anchorage was off the little town of Breves, on the western shore of Marajo Island, and the center of a flourishing rubber business. The inhabitants were doubtless as much surprised at seeing us as were the natives of the West Indies when Columbus' galleys first appeared, since never before had an ocean going ship appeared at Breves.

The next day took us into a long strait hardly wide enough for the ship to pass, and at times it was necessary to brace the yards sharp up, to clear the branches of the great trees that rose some hundred feet above our deck. To one unaccustomed to the luxuriance of the tropics there was something extremely novel and interesting in the passage of two days through this narrow strait, where contact with jungle vegetation and life was necessarily so close and intimate. Had we met another ship there would not have been room to pass. Fortunately there are two of these straits, called "Furos," and the rule is strictly enforced that ascending vessels shall take one passage, and descending vessels the other.

It was late at night when we anchored for the second time within the furos, and as the ship emerged into the broad Amazon on the following morning, feelings were inspired which could never be forgotten. The queen of all rivers in the world was rolling on in resistless majesty. Four miles broad, and stretching out to the westward until lost in the dim outline of the distant horizon, it was more like a sea than a river, even though it did drain half a continent. That this tremendous flow of water, amounting to many millions of cubic feet per minute, could be fed, month by month and year by year, merely by the condensed vapors evaporated from the ocean, and borne overhead in cloud form by the trade winds to the interior, staggered the imagination.

Soon after leaving the delta, machinery troubles began, which were destined to permanently handicap the expedition. We stopped to speak a passing schooner, and on starting ahead again, a loud crash was heard in the engine room, accompanied by an escape of steam up the hatch. The relief valves had failed to operate properly, and condensed water in the cylinders had brought undue strains on the engine. The connecting rod bolts of the after low-pressure cylinder had broken short off, and let the end of the rod into the well; in which position it had been struck by the revolving crank and badly bent. Fortunately no damage was done to the high-pressure cylinder, and by disconnecting the low-pressure cylinder we were able to proceed at reduced speed; though while steaming solely under one cylinder, there was always a danger of having the engine stick "on center" at critical moments.

Our resources for straightening so large a piece of metal as the bent connecting rod, were very inadequate. Nevertheless, since the success of the whole expedition depended upon motive power, the attempt had to be made. Our little forge was placed in the small fore hatch, under the topgallant forecastle, a hearth of brick built around it so as to enlarge the heating area, and the connecting rod hung in chains over it. A moderate heat was applied, and by means of a hydraulic jack, braced against the deck overhead, the rod by slow stages was brought into its original form.

This work required several days; meantime the ship proceeded up river under one cylinder at the rate of about five knots. But the worst was yet to come. After installing the repaired rod, and steaming once more for twenty-four hours with engines whole, the connecting rod bolts again gave way. By shifting them end for end we had managed to utilize them after the first accident, but this second fracture rendered them entirely useless, and we had no spare ones. Our plight was worse than before. To handle the *Enterprise* on the river for any great length of time under one cylinder, would be to endanger her safety, and moreover would consume more time than was at our disposal. It seemed to me that the expedition must fail.

In this emergency one of the machinists, James

Moore, came forward and told me that if the proper size of metal could be found, he felt confident he could cut the necessary threads of the bolts by hand. The ship was searched for pieces of metal of the required three inches in diameter. There were none in the engineer department, but among the ordnance stores was found one bar of 3″ wrought iron, the transporting axle of the eleven inch pivot gun. During the next month, Moore, with the aid of another machinist named Chambers, performed successfully the delicate task of cutting the threads. I do not hesitate to say, that but for their skill the expedition could not have succeeded. On returning to Washington I tried in vain to have Moore commissioned in the Engineer Corps, but in 1880 was able to obtain an appointment for him in a leading civil capacity at the Torpedo Station, Newport. He has since filled that position with eminent satisfaction, during the forty-three years that have intervened.

While Moore and Chambers were laboriously cutting the threads, the *Enterprise* proceeded under one cylinder to the mouth of the Madeira, 800 miles from Para. No permit had arrived, and consequently I was in a quandary. Should the ship return to Para with negative results, and waste valuable time awaiting the permit, or commit a breach of diplomatic etiquette by proceeding up the Madeira and carrying out the work assigned? Inherently the survey would be in no wise a trespass, since it was directly in the interests of Brazil. I concluded to take the bull by the horns and go ahead with the work, leaving it to my superiors to explain. The day after arrival was spent in measuring a base line, and in fixing its north end by stellar observations. Then the ship proceeded up the Madeira River.

On June 21st we reached Uroa Island, 200 miles from the base line. Our pilots declined the responsibility of taking the ship farther, on account of large boulders in the river, and the crippled condition of the machinery forced me to anchor and attempt a survey of the remaining distance of 350 miles with the steam launch. It would be a difficult task against a strong current, for this low powered boat, only 26 feet long, but there was no other alternative. Lieutenant Blocklinger was placed in charge, with Lieutenant Perkins as observer, and Mr. Sparrow to cut in the shore line. The enthusiasm, energy, and perseverance with which they worked reflected great credit upon them.

During the absence of the launch, a boat arrived with a Lieutenant of the Brazilian Navy, who delivered to me a letter from the President of the Province of the Amazons, Baron de Maracaja. The President had learned of our presence in the Madeira, without the permission of the Imperial Government of Brazil, and requested our departure without delay. I replied that my mission was fully understood by his Ambassador at Washington, and that only through some unfortunate delay of which I was ignorant, the necessary visé had not arrived. That repairs were in progress upon the *Enterprise's* engines which were crippled; if, however, upon hearing further from him, my explanation was not satisfactory, I would immediately leave. Mention was omitted, however, of a strong hope that we could complete our survey work before an answer from him could be received!

Several days later the boiler of the steam launch broke down completely, after 300 miles of river had been surveyed. Fifty more miles remained to the head of navigation at San Antonio. I boarded a passing river steamer for the scene of the breakdown, and arranged with the captain to permit me to complete the survey during his passage to San Antonio and return. On reaching the launch Lieutenant Perkins joined me, and together we accomplished the remainder of the work very well, the captain of the steamer, the *Canuman,* kindly giving us every facility for soundings and observations. Life on board these river steamers proved very cosmopolitan. No staterooms or berths were provided, as no person in that country traveled without his "rede," a grass hammock which was hung in whatever part of the upper deck that best suited the owner. It was a cleanly plan, well adapted to the climate, for berths would have been intolerably hot and alive with vermin. A separate apartment was reserved for women.

Upon my return to the *Enterprise* the engine repairs had been completed, and on July 22nd we sailed for the Amazon. The expedition had successfully accomplished its principal mission, in determining that ocean steamers of 22 feet draft can navigate the Madeira with safety, from its mouth to the Falls of San Antonio, 578 miles above; except from the middle of July to the following January, when the lack of rainfall causes a decided lowering of the river level. From January to June the least depth is about six fathoms.

It had been very arduous work in a hot, moist climate, averaging 87 degrees during the day, though the nights were not uncomfortable. On two days a cool wind from the southwest brought a most disagreeable drop in the thermometer to 70 degrees, and we were all searching for blankets. But even the normal heat caused us less discomfort than the insects; swarms of sand flies, "piums," during the day would be succeeded by equally numerous mosquitoes at night. There was little sickness on the ship, though the appearance of the Europeans who lived ashore, was sufficient evidence of the notoriously unhealthy conditions created by the great stretches of swamps in the San Antonio vicinity. I have never seen more sickly or unhappy looking men than the laborers on the railroad. Hardly a single one had escaped the fevers, and their pale and cadaverous appearance was pitiable. We were fortunate to get away from this country before the onset of the rainy season.[1]

Climatic conditions prevented the completion of the railroad for many years, notwithstanding the utilization of the Madeira, after our survey, for transporting supplies by ocean steamers. The very unhealthy conditions of life ashore caused the death of such a large proportion of the construction force that several successive efforts were necessary before the line was finally opened in about 1921. Now this route taps a remote country, adjacent to 900 miles of navigable waters above the Falls of the Madeira River.

July 24th found the *Enterprise* again on the Amazon River. The desirability of making some apologies to the President of the Province for having entered the Madeira without a permit, took us seventy-five miles out of our course to the town of Manaos, at the mouth of the Rio Negro. The President received my explanations very graciously, and we parted with the best of understandings.

During all of the passage down the Amazon, the ship was busily engaged in making a running survey of that great river. This work did not require the exactitude of the Madeira survey, because

---

[1] In 1873 the rainfall at San Antonio as observed by an English engineer was as follows:

Jan. 15″.85	April 11″.01	July 0″.32	Oct. 1″.98
Feb. 10″.87	May 5″.96	Aug. 1″.07	Nov. 11″.32
Mar. 14″.89	June 2″.56	Sept. 5″.70	Dec. 10″.08

there was no question of ample draft of water at all seasons for navigational purposes, from the mouth of the Negro River (about sixty miles above the Madeira's mouth) to the sea. The method adopted was to steam at a regular rate of speed for a distance of about 25 miles each day, taking repeated bearings from the ship of prominent objects along the banks. Two lines of soundings were made, one by the *Enterprise* and the other by the steam launch, whose positions were determined by angling on the ship. To the data thus obtained, corrections for current and geographical positions were applied from information gained each night at the anchorage. There the rate of the current was determined, and stellar observations taken for precise latitude and longitude. The altitude of the river at various points was ascertained by noting the height of the mercurial barometer, which was subsequently compared with the record of a similar instrument left at Para, and kindly read by our Consul, Mr. Andrew Cahn. In this way the work progressed rapidly, and with sufficient accuracy for the intended purpose.

The more we learned of the Amazon, the greater were we impressed with its immensity. At Serpa, 800 miles from the ocean, the cross section was very favorable to a determination of the volume of discharge. Here the river narrows to a mile in width, with straight, steep banks on both sides, and a uniform current. A depth of 330 feet was found in mid-channel. Notwithstanding that it was August, and the river level 6 feet below high water, our observations recorded the astonishing total discharge of 3,850,000 cubic feet per second. At the origin of the delta, 200 miles from the sea, the Amazon divides into two great branches, each of them as large as the Mississippi River, and below this point several large tributaries enter, whose combined flow at certain seasons might make almost a third Mississippi. The average width of the Amazon, from the mouth of the Negro River to the delta is about $2\frac{1}{2}$ miles, and in the rainy season from November until early Spring, this is greatly increased by numerous inundations, forming large lakes for many miles back from the banks. These drain but slowly, and hence serve a useful purpose in stabilizing the water level, and rendering the river navigable to large ships at all seasons. It is not only in its width and great volume of flow that the Amazon exceeds all other rivers in the world, but also in its astonishing depths. Not less than 60 feet prevails in the channel as far up as the Rio Negro, if not farther.

Most geographers consider the mouth of the Amazon as being 180 miles wide, but this could be true only on the basis of including Marajo Bay, which in my opinion is really an arm of the sea into which the Pará River empties. Though Marajo Bay is connected with the Amazon by lagoons and estuaries, their characteristics, and the intervention of the large island of Marajo, seem to forbid their inclusion as a part of the great river. I consider that the delta may be justly said to comprise only the waters to the northward of Marajo Island, and hence to have a width of about 100 miles.

About half way down the Amazon a stop was made at Santarem, beautifully situated on rising ground near the mouth of the Tapajoz River. This town particularly interested me because it had been a settlement of American families, who had emigrated after the Civil War, feeling that they could no longer live under the "Stars and Stripes." Sickness, and the difficulty of adjustment to the life of the natives, caused them so much dissatisfaction, that later they were glad to accept the offer of our government to send the *Quinnebaug* to return them to the United States. While at Santarem my attention was called to the situation of a poor little orphan girl named Alice Scope, whose American parents had died, leaving her in the care of a native foster mother. With the consent of the latter, I determined to rescue the little waif and took her on board the *Enterprise*.

We reached Para on August 31st, after an absence of three months, having completed a running survey of 1,500 miles. The Judge of the Orphan Court there objected to my taking Alice Scope, and ordered her return to Santarem, but I ignored the protest by simply turning the correspondence over to the American Consul before sailing. Meantime the latter's wife was good enough to do my shopping in outfitting the poor waif, who had no clothes except the little calico slip she stood in. Alice was quite uncivilized. She ate with her fingers, and in general behaved as a savage might be expected to do, but she was very bright and engaging, and soon became a great favorite on board.

Upon arrival at New York I communicated with her relatives in Texas, whose address had been given me by the native foster mother, and they asked to have Alice sent to them by steamer. She cried bitterly when the time came to leave the *Enterprise,* and the whole ship's company regretted to see her go. The relatives notified me of her safe arrival in Texas, but I have never heard of Alice since, and have always been sorry not to know something more of her subsequent life.

The writer took the first opportunity to go to Washington, where, through the Secretary of the Navy, the Secretary of State was asked why the permit for the navigation of the Madeira River had not been sent to the *Enterprise.* In reply the State Department regretted very much that my original request, made before starting for Brazil, to obtain this necessary authority had been overlooked, and never taken up with the Brazilian Government! It was indeed fortunate that I had not awaited permission to enter the Madeira River before undertaking the survey; nearly a year would have been lost.

On making my report of the survey to the Secretary of the Navy, Hon. R. W. Thompson, he was kind enough to express his congratulations upon the success of the expedition, and to show his appreciation in a practical way by assigning the *Enterprise* to the very desirable European Station.

CHAPTER XXI

THE "ENTERPRISE'S" CRUISE IN EUROPE

COMPARED with the arduous nature of nearly all my previous service afloat, the cruise of a year and a half on the *Enterprise* in European waters was almost like yachting. It was my first opportunity to visit the famous places of the Old World, to enjoy their beautiful scenes and works of art, to sense the inspiration of their historical associations, and to meet many persons of eminence, including royalty. Altogether this cruise crowded in more experiences of pleasant personal interest than any other corresponding period of my career.

But it was not all pure enjoyment. Notwithstanding the ship's reputation of "the lucky little *Enterprise,*" bad weather dogged her course from departure in November of 1878 until return to the United States in the Spring of 1880. On the outward passage from New York gale after gale was encountered, and near the meridian of the Azores we picked up one which blew steadily from the eastward for twelve days. During most of this time we were "hove to" under only a close reefed main topsail, and when the squalls were especially hard it was even necessary to substitute a main trysail. Fortunately she was a weatherly little craft and rarely did seas come aboard, but heavy rolling, frequently as great as 45 degrees, made the thirty-seven day trip tiresome and uncomfortable.

This experience was especially novel and trying for my family, who had taken passage on board, by the kind permission of the Secretary of the Navy. In spite of the weather it was a great pleasure to have them with me, rather than to endure another of the long separations so common to the life of a naval officer. One episode incidental to their being on board, however, might well have cost me a permanent separation from my wife, but for her exceptionally generous nature. Among the rings which Mrs. Selfridge was wearing was her engagement ring and a four carat diamond solitaire. The latter was especially valuable, both intrinsically and from its association with her father, who had bought it as the best means of investing and securing his savings, while Military Governor of Louisiana during the Civil War. My wife was in the habit of allowing her jewelry to stand for several hours in a tumbler of soapy water, as a preliminary to its periodic cleaning. One morning my passion for tidiness, inherited from New England ancestry, and heightened by long naval training, was offended by the sight of the tumbler of dirty looking water standing on a shelf in the cabin. I could not resist the impulse to hastily toss the water out of the port-hole, a glimpse of the glittering jewels coming too late to save them from the depths of 3000 fathoms!

On reaching Ville Franche in December, the Commander-in-Chief, Admiral Le Roy, issued orders for the *Enterprise* to cruise in the eastern Mediterranean, touching at various ports going and returning. The beauty of the Bay of Naples, the first stop, was a delight to me, then and ever afterwards. Whether coming from the north around Ischia, or from the south past Capua, the setting given to Mount Vesuvius with its never failing cloud of smoke, exceeds in beauty that of any other of the numerous ports of the world that I have visited. We took the opportunity to "do" this veritable sightseer's paradise; of course including a visit to Capri's blue grotto, the Temple of Theseus, the crater of Vesuvius, and other well known places in this great center of interest and beauty. Before sailing, I bade a reluctant farewell to my wife and the boys who left for Florence.

From Naples the ship proceeded to Alexandria, where advantage was taken of the chance to visit Cairo, the Pyramids, the Mosque of Omar, and to take a trip up the Nile, by river steamer. The next port of call was Joppa, Palestine, but so much time had been spent in Alexandria that we could not tarry longer than to permit the officers and crew, in quarter watches, to spend two days in Jerusalem. At Beirut we were warmly welcomed by the President and faculty of the American College, who emphasized the value of our visit in ameliorating their many annoying misunderstandings with the Turkish authorities. On this account I was not sorry to remain longer than had been planned, and the delay enabled me and many of the officers to visit Baalbek and Damascus, to which latter point the French had constructed a narrow gauge railway, over the Lebanon range of mountains. Damascus had to rest on its ancient laurels, for we found merely a shabby, dirty Turkish town with nothing of special interest. Baalbek, however, reached after a two hours' horseback ride from the railroad, well repaid our trouble. The Temple of the Sun is an astonishing example of the extraordinary skill of the ancient builders, and in this respect is quite comparable to the Pyramids of Egypt. The foundations of this temple are immense blocks of solid stone, several feet above the ground, which are said to weigh more than 1000 tons each. What means were employed to put such great weights in their lofty place probably never will be known.

From Beirut the *Enterprise* coasted along Anatolia to Smyrna, where we found little of special interest. Through the American Minister at Constantinople permission was obtained to pass the historic Dardanelles to the ancient capital of Constantinople, and after a somewhat lengthy and exceedingly interesting stay, the *Enterprise* proceeded to Pireus, the seaport of Athens. Finally, the five months swing around the Mediterranean was ended by arrival at Ville Franche, where I reported to the new Commander-in-Chief, Rear Admiral John C. Howell, and obtained a short leave to visit my family in Florence.

At this time I was delighted to receive an invitation from Ferdinand de Lesseps, the eminent French engineer who had built the Suez Canal, to attend as a delegate an Interoceanic Congress which was to assemble in Paris in the following June, under the auspices of the Geographic Society of France. De Lesseps' success at Suez had led him to look for "new worlds to conquer," and to his sending two French engineers to the isthmus between the Atlantic and Pacific Oceans, to examine the possibilities of a canal there. They chose the easiest method of examination, by merely going over the Panama Railroad, and on their return reported this line as the best in existence. The congress was especially to consider the recommendations of these two French engineers, but my Darien survey reports were accessible to De Lesseps, and he included that route in the agenda. Admiral Howell kindly arranged a northern itinerary for the *Enterprise,* and gave permission for her to stop at Havre while the congress was in session.

The ship reached Havre in May, 1879, and

after mooring her to the quay, in view of the prospective long stay, the writer went to Paris. Vice-Admiral De La Roncière-de-Noury, President of the Geographic Society of France, presided over the congress which was attended by many of the most distinguished civil engineers of Europe. My report on the Darien surveys was referred to one of the principal committees, and I was afforded sufficient opportunity to present arguments in favor of the Atrato-Napipi route, assisted by an English gentleman who was a fluent French scholar. To another committee Rear Admiral Ammen, U. S. N., assisted by Civil Engineer Menocal, argued for the Nicaraguan route. But it was evident from the beginning that the general sentiment of the congress favored a sea level canal. De Lesseps' opinion necessarily carried great weight, and he would accept no other route than that of Panama.

However the congress generously recognized that my elimination of many routes across the Darien Isthmus had greatly simplified its deliberations. At the close, Mons. Le Febrese de Foury, the senior engineer of the committee to which my plans had been submitted, made an address in a plenary session and paid me the following compliments:—

"The project by way of the Atrato is one that has been made very enticing by the devotion of the man who has more especially occupied himself with this question. (Applause.)

"I believe I am the interpreter of the commission in saying that Mr. Selfridge will carry away with him the admiration of the commission (applause), and I do not for a moment doubt that the entire commission will agree to the words with which I have expressed my high appreciation of the beautiful work of Commander Selfridge." (Prolonged applause.)

Subsequently the French Government bestowed upon me the decoration of Chevalier of the National Order of the Legion of Honor.[1]

Sailing from Havre the *Enterprise* proceeded on the northern itinerary and arrived at Antwerp

---

[1] Its receipt was acknowledged by the following letter:

"VICE-ADMIRAL DE LA RONCIERÉ-DE-NOURY,
 SENATOR, PRESIDENT GEOGRAPHICAL
  SOCIETY OF FRANCE, PARIS.

SIR:

I have the honor to acknowledge yours of July 1st just received, in which you inform me, that agreeably to your solicitation the Government of France has bestowed upon me the decoration of Chevalier of the National Order of the Legion of Honor.

Permit me, my dear Admiral, to thank you for such generous appreciation of my work upon the Isthmus of Darien and to express my gratitude for the very high honor that the Government of France has considered me worthy to receive.

With sentiments of deep respect for yourself personally,
 I remain

> Very truly
> THOS. O. SELFRIDGE
> Commander,
> United States Navy."

without incident. There the services of a well recommended English North Sea pilot were
engaged, and he accompanied us on the trip to
Wilhelmshaven—ultimately to my sorrow. He
came within an ace of grounding the ship on the
dangerous shoals which extend a long distance
from the German coast off the Weser River.
Here the bottom is of shifting sands, which, with
even a moderate sea running, will silt over a
stranded vessel in a few hours, and if the *Enterprise* had touched the ground under the weather
condition prevailing at the time in question, she
would undoubtedly have been rolled over, and
buried in the sands.

We had been running all day before a fresh
breeze under topsails and courses, frequently cutting our course to avoid Dutch fishermen as they
loomed up in the mist which prevented even a
glimpse of the low coast. Sitting at the open port
in the cabin, I was startled by a wave "combing"
and breaking under the counter, and at this evidence of shallow water I ran on deck and warned
the pilot on the bridge. He replied with confidence
"I know where we are." Following my long standing rule not to interfere with a pilot, especially
since this one had been so highly recommended for
those waters, I returned to the cabin. Presently
another sea broke, and then believing that there
was no time to be lost, again I rushed on deck,
and this time ignoring the pilot, called to the officer

of the watch to send the men aft to the braces, and to the quartermaster to jump into the main chains and get a cast of the lead.

Anxiously I watched the quartermaster's heave. Observing that the lead landed well forward and that there was much slack line to be hauled in, I did not wait for the result but "sang out," "Hard down the helm, brace sharp up." The quartermaster reported 3½ fathoms (21 feet); leaving a dangerously small margin of only three feet. We all held our breath, while the ship responded slowly to the dispositions of helm and sails which would take her farther off shore. The next cast of the lead gave the same depth as before, 3½ fathoms, but the third cast indicated a deepening to 4 fathoms and relieved the extreme tenseness of the situation. Then, turning to the pilot, I could not restrain some old-fashioned nautical phraseology in ordering him off the bridge, where I took charge. A few minutes longer on the old course would have been the end of the *Enterprise.* It was one of those narrow escapes which come to every sailor, and are inseparable from naval service, but it taught me a valuable lesson. With or without a pilot the commanding officer should never give up control of the navigation of his ship. Throughout my subsequent career afloat I trusted only to the lead when on soundings, and the position was uncertain, and acted promptly on my own judgment even if it conflicted with a pilot's advice.

The next morning, at the lightship off the mouth of the Jade River, no local pilot could be found, and we had to feel the way through a dense fog with both leads going. It was a great relief finally to pick up the faint tinkle of the bell buoy that marked the outer end of a well-buoyed channel up the river, to the dockyard at Wilhelmshaven. This was one of the most important of the German naval bases, and the authorities were very polite in showing us about. We noted many examples of German efficiency in preparation, which of course were the subject of a report to Admiral Howell. Leaving Wilhelmshaven, we touched at Cuxhaven to land the demoted pilot, who felt his disgrace keenly.

The next stop was at Christiania, at the head of a beautiful fiord. The kind American consul, Mr. Gader, took several parties of officers on very interesting and delightful tours through Norway, traveling partly by post carriages and partly by lake steamers. It was with much regret that we sailed away. At Copenhagen we were treated most courteously by the Danish naval authorities. They had some Whitehead (automobile) torpedoes which interested us very much, as the old-fashioned spar and towing torpedoes had not then been displaced. A full report upon the Whitehead trials, given for our benefit, was made to the Bureau of Ordnance.

The ship reached Cronstadt on July 15th, and the visit was made memorable by numerous attentions to both officers and crew by the kind Russians whose hospitality seemed inexhaustible. A splendid steamer was placed at our disposal for trips to St. Petersburg. By special invitation the crew visited the palace grounds at Peterhof, where the beautiful fountains, fully equal to those of Versailles, were put in play for their benefit. On invitation I paid my respects, accompanied by my staff, to the Grand Duke Constantine, the head of the Russian Navy, at his palace in St. Petersburg. I found him not only thoroughly conversant in all nautical matters, but also keen to keep in touch with naval developments. He returned my call promptly and was received on the *Enterprise* with all the honors due to his exalted rank. The following day I breakfasted with His Highness at the residence of the governor of Cronstadt, Vice-Admiral Kasakevitch. The Grand Duke and myself talked a good deal of shop, and he kept several aides flying about bringing plans and papers as he wanted them.

On the occasion of the Emperor's birthday, July 30th, the Russian fleet held a review in his honor. The position assigned the *Enterprise* was between the two long columns of ships. I had inquired of the Governor whether the Tsar would visit the *Enterprise,* but he could not give a definite answer and advised being prepared. Consequently we were not taken by surprise when the royal barge was seen to head in our direction after leaving the

Russian flagship, and Alexander III was received with full honors prescribed by regulations, and a little more, as a special recognition of the first time that an Emperor of Russia had visited an American man-of-war. He was followed on board by Grand Dukes and other persons of high rank, so numerous that the port gangway had to be utilized in addition to the starboard.

The Tsar, a tall handsome man, dressed in the full uniform of an Admiral, came first into the cabin and sipped a glass of wine. He spoke English very well, and seemed pleased at the opportunity of paying an attention to our "Great American Republic," as he styled it. Withal he seemed sad, as though pressed with the cares and responsibilities of reigning; an attitude doubtless reflected from an undercurrent of civic unrest, manifested not many months afterwards by his being killed by a bomb exploded under his carriage. From the cabin the Emperor walked around and inspected the upper decks, and then took a departure marked by the customary ceremonies of manning the yards and firing a 21-gun salute.

Not the least of many pleasant incidents of my stay in Russia, was the opportunity of seeing my sister Kate, who was living in St. Petersburg after marrying Captain Etholin of the Russian Imperial Navy.

On the day before sailing, the officers of Cronstadt gave our officers the compliment of a dinner,

which passed off with great éclat—one end of the
long table, where the juniors made merry was
dubbed the "forecastle," while the center, where a
more dignified behavior prevailed, was called the
"quarterdeck." The sailors of the Russian fleet
gave our crew a similar send-off dinner.

Before sailing I addressed a letter to Admiral
Kasakevitch, Governor of Cronstadt,[1] in an attempt to express my very genuine appreciation of
the extraordinary hospitality which had been extended to us while in Cronstadt. As we steamed
out of the harbor the Admiral of the Dock Yard
paid us the final unusual compliment of accompany-
ing the ship for several miles in his steam barge.

> "U. S. S. 'ENTERPRISE'
> CRONSTADT, RUSSIA.
> July 31, 1879.

SIR:

Upon leaving Russia, I desire to express to your Excellency my
thanks and deep appreciation of the many courtesies, official and
unofficial, that have been extended to us by yourself and officers
of the Imperial Navy, and which I have already communicated to
my Government.

I have felt keenly the honor paid to my Country by the visits
of His Majesty the Emperor, and His Highness the Grand Duke,
and will you do me the favor to communicate to His Highness my
best wishes for his prosperity and that of the Imperial family.

With kindest regards to Madam Kasakevitch,

I have the honor to be, Sir,

> Very respectfully,
> THOS. O. SELFRIDGE,
> Commander,
> Comdg.

ADMIRAL KASAKEVITCH,
GOVERNOR OF CRONSTADT,
CRONSTADT."

It had been one of the most interesting and enjoyable experiences of my life, and the evidences of friendship for America, universally displayed by the Russians on this occasion, were manifestly sincere.[1]

After leaving the Baltic via Kiel, the *Enterprise* went to Cowes, Isle of Wight, where Queen Victoria was occupying her summer palace of Osborne House. It had long been my desire to meet the Queen, and one day I took advantage of a conversation with Captain Frank Thompson, commanding the royal yacht, to ask if it could be

[1] In the following report I called Admiral Howell's attention to the Russian sentiments towards us:—

"U. S. S. 'ENTERPRISE'
CRONSTADT, RUSSIA.
July 30, 1879.

SIR:

It gives me pleasure to be able to report to the Commander-in-Chief the great courtesy, official and unofficial, that has been extended to this ship by Admiral Kasakevitch, the Governor of Cronstadt, and his staff.

Upon expressing my desire to inspect the torpedo defenses of the Russian Navy, except such as were considered secret, he replied, "With pleasure, we have no secrets from Americans." This I am informed is a compliment that has never before been permitted any representative of a foreign government.

In company with other officers I have inspected the torpedo equipment now in use and will make it the subject of a special report. I shall also upon invitation visit tomorrow the iron-clad battery of Cronstadt Harbor.

I have the honor to be, Sir,

Very respectfully,
Your ob'd't servant
THOS. O. SELFRIDGE,
Commander,
Comdg."

arranged. He said that he would make enquiries of some members of the royal household whom he was soon due to bring from Southampton, and that meantime I should call at the lodge at the gates of the palace and subscribe by name in the visitor's book. The Queen was said to be so much interested in knowing whom of her loyal subjects took the trouble to call at the lodge, that she inspected the visitor's book every morning. If she did so she found my name therein.

Not long afterwards a note was received from Lord Ponsonby, stating that the Queen would be pleased to receive me at a certain time, and adding his invitation to lunch with the royal household. On the appointed day it was pouring rain, and a stiff breeze made a very choppy sea in the open road-stead of Cowes. But the opportunity of being presented to Queen Victoria was too rare to be neglected, so packing my special full-dress uniform in water-tight bags, and dressing myself in oilskins, I braved the atrocious weather in the gig.

At a hotel on shore I changed into proper uniform, hired a carriage, and set forth a lone visitor for the palace. The driver left me at the main door, which was open and led into a long corridor. There was no one to receive me nor could I find a door bell. Apparently, at her summer residence the Queen discarded those forms of royalty which forbade anyone presenting himself unless by special orders, yet I was reluctant to enter too unceremoniously. My problem, which for a time seemed to leave no alternative but to storm the castle, was finally solved by the appearance of a lackey in the distance. He speedily rushed off and presently brought back a message from Lord Ponsonby, who soon appeared in person.

The luncheon was rather stiff. There were present some elderly ladies, whom I supposed to be maids of honor or ladies-in-waiting, and some of the gentlemen of the Court. But they had little to say to one another. After luncheon Lord Ponsonby said, "Captain, I think we can see the Queen now," and accompanied me to the drawing room. While we were conversing there, he suddenly whispered, "The Queen." Turning, I saw a rather stout lady, plainly dressed in black, advancing all alone.

Going up to the Queen at once, I thanked Her Majesty for the honor of the presentation. She replied that she was always glad to see Americans, and then, laughing about the weather said, "See what America sends us!" "Yes, Your Majesty, England gives good for evil, for my country will always remember the active interest of the late Prince Consort in our Civil War." This answer seemed to please her, and after a little more desultory conversation, my departure was made in the conventional manner of backing from the royal presence, out of the room. Thus ended my interview with Queen Victoria, the one person in royal circles whom I had been anxious to meet. On taking my leave of Lord Ponsonby he was kind enough to say, "Captain, you were cut out for a courtier."

Some days later the Prince of Wales (afterwards King Edward VII) visited the *Enterprise,* and, notwithstanding his previous designation of the call as "informal," was received with full honors; which included the assembly of all hands at quarters, the manning of the rail and yards, etc. Just as he came over the gangway, with everyone at a salute, the wind caught his cap and blew it overboard. But he was quite equal to the occasion, and took the incident very humorously, thus living up to his reputation for good nature and quick-wittedness. As is well known the Prince had a most engaging personality. He made himself very agreeable on board, displayed a keen interest in various features of the ship, and in differences which he noted between minor customs in the British Navy and our own, and generally proved himself to be well informed in naval matters.

The itinerary took the *Enterprise* back to Ville Franche in October, 1879, and the remainder of the cruise was spent in the Mediterranean until departure for home. During this period I had an interesting and personally very gratifying experience with one of the boats which had been built according to my father's design, as mentioned in the first chapter. This boat belonged to the *Quinnebaug* and had finished a bad "last" in a pulling race between all the cutters of the squadron, held while the *Enterprise* was in northern Europe. It had been transferred to the *Alliance,* bound for home, in exchange for the winner of the race, a sharp, narrow cutter.

Loyalty to my father, and belief in the excellence of his design, moved me to request the further transfer of the then unpopular boat to the *Enterprise,* to replace our racing cutter which had been lost in one of the numerous gales that pursued us. Our race-boat crew had made a fine record in their old boat, and were not pleased to see *Black Maria,* as they dubbed her, come on board. She was built for general ship's use, rather than racing; but fine entrance lines, a broad bilge, and a hollow floor, all tended to make a speedy boat, and faith in her determined me to prove her worth, notwithstanding the prejudice of our crew.

I went in her on the first try-out, and observed what apparently no one else had noticed, that the rowlocks were too narrow to permit a full swing of the oars. This was remedied by larger rowlocks, and then the problem was to gain the confidence of the racing crew in their boat. It is not easy to remove the prejudice of sailors; they can be forced to man a boat, but not to put their hearts into pulling it. A few months later, at Alexandria, I handled the *Black Maria* in a sailing race between all the boats of the ship, and came in a good first, and with so much prestige gained, called the race-boat crew aft and had a talk with them. After explaining the reason for the boat's defeat in the squadron pulling race (narrow rowlocks), I said to them, "Boys, I want you to change her name to *Sweet Maria*. When we reach Pireus I will measure off a mile course, and if you will beat your record for that distance made in your old cutter, I will give you an extra 24 hours liberty."

At Pireus, after a week's training by Ensign Hunt to get the crew into condition, they lowered their old record over the measured mile by a half minute. Then the crew came to me and said, "Captain, the boat is all right, and we are ready to pull and bet on her." They were promised a chance, and upon arrival at Ville Franche I explained to Admiral Howell our eagerness for a race with the *Quinnebaug,* the ship whose racing crew had been glad to discard *Black Maria,* and now possessed the boat which had won the Squadron race. He was a good sport, and replied laughingly, "I will give you an opportunity." The *Enterprise* was soon en route for Naples, on some public matter, with orders to stop at Leghorn on the return. At Naples, we fell in with one of our ships whose cutter had come in second in the squadron race. *Black Maria* gave that boat a good beating, which made us more than ever keen to take on the *Quinnebaug's* boat.

Within a few hours of the *Enterprise* anchoring at Leghorn, *Black Maria* tossed oars under the bows of the *Quinnebaug*—the time honored challenge for a race. Those on the *Quinnebaug* could not believe that their old beaten discard was in earnest, and were more than glad to accept the challenge, and to consent to the condition of a four mile race, which would more certainly make the result depend upon the qualities of the respective boats. On the day of the race the breakwater at Leghorn was crowded with spectators, principally the friends of the officers of the *Quinnebaug*, which had been under repairs in that port for several months. It was an anxious time for the few, comparatively friendless, "rooters" of the *Enterprise*, until my binoculars sighted *Black Maria* coming along beautifully far in the lead. That the *Quinnebaug's* crew were doing their best was evidenced by their splashing badly, while our men rowed as smoothly as at practice. My triumph was complete when the boat of my father's design, renamed *Sweet Maria*, came in victorious by a half mile.

It was a stunning defeat for the *Quinnebaug*, and Captain Farquhar could scarcely believe that nothing had been done to the boat except to enlarge the rowlocks, and relieve the crew from pulling as in strait jackets. *Sweet Maria* subsequently won many races, both abroad and at home, and became a famous boat, but was finally beaten, probably as the result of having a poor crew. Certainly she had amply demonstrated the excellence of a design, whose ultimate discard I have always ascribed to the prejudice of certain naval constructors against the efforts of line officers in such matters.

During the last visit to Pireus, mentioned above, I had the honor of dining with the King and Queen of Greece at their palace in Athens. It was a large formal state dinner, where my rank forbade sitting very near either of Their Majesties, but after it was over the King paid the very polite compliment to each of his guests, of going around and speaking to them individually. King George was a tall, handsome man with a fine military carriage and a gracious address. Like all the crowned heads whom I have met, he was full of inquiries about America, doubtless due in part to the fact that so many of his subjects had emigrated there.

I also had a very pleasant talk with Queen Olga. She was interested to hear news of her father, the Grand Duke Constantine, whom I had seen during my recent visit to Cronstadt, and graciously accepted an invitation to visit the *Enterprise* on the following day. She came without the King, but accompanied by one of her ladies and her naval aide-de-camp. After a cup of tea in the cabin, where some of the wardroom officers assisted me, the Queen walked about the ship, and chatted in a very democratic way with a number of the bluejackets. Altogether she left a most agreeable impression on the little ship which she had honored with her presence.

The *Enterprise* sailed for the United States in April, 1880, and I was much gratified to be allowed the privilege of taking my family home in her. Most of the passage was made under sail, the "northeast trades" being followed for westings. Twenty-five days took us to Hampton Roads, whence we proceeded up the Chesapeake and Potomac to Washington, for final inspection and decommissioning. It had been an exceedingly varied and interesting cruise.

CHAPTER XXII

ASHORE AND AFLOAT

WHEN the *Enterprise* was placed out of commission in 1880, her captain was given a short leave, and then reported as a member of the class of instruction in torpedoes, mines, chemistry, and electricity, at the Naval Torpedo Station, Newport, Rhode Island. The course was of great value, and I have always considered it a mistake to abandon the long standing practice of sending officers to these special classes.

In 1881 I was much gratified to begin a four year detail in command of the Torpedo Station, where the largely scientific nature of the work proved intensely interesting. At that period the Whitehead torpedo, smokeless powder, gun cotton, and electric light and power, were in their infancy, and on the eve of general introduction into the Navy, where they have all since played such important parts. The Torpedo Station was the cradle of their naval development, and the experimental and research work incident thereto occupied a great part of my time, and was highly attractive to me.

The most conspicuous incident of my four years at Newport was the visit of President Arthur, accompanied by the Secretary of the Navy, and members of the Senate Naval Committee, during which some torpedo firing was conducted for the President's benefit. The climax was the intentional destruction of the antequated light-house tender *Joseph Henry*. While mechanically controlled from the shore by an electrical device invented by Lieutenant T. C. McLean, the vessel was blown up by a spar torpedo. Upon the conclusion of the demonstration the President was kind enough to congratulate me upon its success.

While at Newport, in 1881, the very acceptable step in promotion from the rank of Commander to that of Captain, was attained, and in 1885 a new cruise was begun by orders to command the *Omaha*. This vessel had been recently rebuilt on entirely new lines. In those days Congress would not appropriate money for new ships, though funds were made available to repair the rapidly deteriorating relics of the Civil War. It was not unusual to practically reconstruct an old vessel, from the keel up, the new ship containing scarcely a timber of the old, and taking on a radically different appearance. This had been done to the *Omaha*, and with great success, as she was a fine sailer and a strikingly handsome vessel—a captain in the British Navy once said to me that she was the handsomest ship he had ever seen. Her principal deficiency was a small coal supply, which made it necessary to keep her under canvas nearly all the time while at sea.

Before leaving the United States the new ship was visited by the Secretary of the Navy, and at the conclusion of an inspection which greatly pleased him, I sought to complete a successful occasion by offering the Secretary a glass of champagne. When the wine was served I was disturbed to note that there was no "fizz" in the glasses, and feared that my new stock, acquired in anticipation of a long cruise abroad, might be flat. Just as the Secretary started drinking from his glass, the truth flashed into my mind. While at Newport my wife had made some apple-jack, put it in empty champagne bottles, and sent it along with my sea stores. In the dark wine locker on board ship, the steward had mistaken one of these bottles for champagne, but it was too late to correct him. Since apple-jack cannot be drunk with the same impunity as champagne, it doubtless burned the Secretary's throat, for he exclaimed, "My! but this is strong champagne." The awkwardness of an explanation persuaded me to not enlighten him, and I have often wondered whether he assumed that the popularly supposed fondness of sailors for strong drink led to their use of extra strong champagne.

The *Omaha's* cruise contained little of special interest, beyond the ordinary peace activities of a man-of-war, and need not be described in detail herein. We made a quick passage of 17 days, only one of them under steam, to Gibraltar, where the quarantine against smallpox caused us to proceed, without anchoring, to Naples. In the Red Sea a favorable northerly wind, unusual for the season, enabled us to set the studdingsails; the last time, to my knowledge, that they were ever used in the American Navy, except on a practice ship. In due course we reached the Orient, where the remainder of the time was spent in the usual visits to Chinese and Japanese ports.

One morning while approaching Nagasaki, I decided to hold target practice, since the ship was required to conduct this exercise every quarter, and but a few days remained of the allotted period. As is usual in those waters native junks and fishing boats were scattered everywhere about the horizon, and at first no place could be found which would be free from the danger of hitting them. A perpendicular cliff, several hundred feet high, near the end of an island upon which no evidences of human habitation could be seen, appeared to offer the best solution of the difficulty. Accordingly the target was anchored close to the island, where the cliff would serve as a backstop for all "overs" and "ricochets." During the subsequent firing the extra precaution was taken of stationing a man aloft, and another in a boat abreast the target, to observe and report whether all shells burst properly on striking the water or cliff. They so reported at the conclusion of the practice, and after picking up the target we proceeded to Nagasaki, confident that no damage had been done, and that no unexploded shells remained behind.

However, after the ship's departure, some Japanese inhabitants came from the other side of the cliff, and at its base found several shells that had not exploded. One of these men was a workman in the arsenal near Nagasaki, and in attempting to explain the intricacies of the shell to his companions, he exploded it, either by striking the fuse or trying to extract it. The poor fellow was killed, together with several others standing about.

On learning of the accident I took the *Omaha* back to the island, and made such amends as were possible, including the distribution to the families of the injured of about $600, which the officers and crew of the *Omaha* had contributed. At that period the Japanese were like the Chinese, in not being very jealous of their international *amour propre,* and the Commander-in-Chief, through the American Minister could have easily adjusted the matter with the local authorities; especially since it was one of those strange pranks of chance where accident follows from the very fact of extra precaution. However, he saw fit to magnify the incident, to detach me from command of the ship without any hearing, and to order me to Washington. On arrival there I found the Secretary of the Navy rather provoked at the Admiral's hasty and drastic action, and I was ordered back to Japan, and the Admiral was instructed to hold a formal inquiry.

As is usual with many such inquiries, the findings were inconclusive. No culpability was attached to my actions, yet I was not specifically relieved from blame. This did not satisfy me. So much had been made over the affair that I wished a complete exoneration on my official record, and this could be obtained only as the outcome of a court martial. After waiting several months in vain for the Secretary to act, I wrote to some friends at home and asked them to bring the matter to a head. Following their interview with the Secretary he ordered a court, with Admiral Jouett as president, and ten other high ranking officers as members. The finding of this court by unanimous vote, was an "Honorable acquittal."

In the *Omaha*, and afterwards, I followed my previous practice of giving special attention to the apprentices. Their quarters were segregated as much as possible from those of the older men, many of whom were rather rough characters in those days. The top-gallant and royal yards were manned almost exclusively by apprentices, who also formed the crew of my gig, and later my barge. Whenever I had the boat wait for me while ashore, the crew (except the boatkeeper) were allowed to land, being required only to be back before the time appointed for my return, and rarely were any of them missing. They became quite proud of pulling the captain, or admiral, and generally responded well to the special care and responsibility given them. The old apprentice system, which included eighteen months at a training station, with a three months' practice cruise before detail to regular service, gave the Navy some of the best petty officers it has ever had. I am sorry to see the system in abeyance now, and believe that it should be restored.

In the *Omaha,* I also tried the experiment of following the British custom of requiring the crew to go barefooted, except on Sundays. It had the manifest advantages of healthfulness and cleanliness, and was much safer and more efficient in work aloft. A bare foot will cling to a footrope when a shoe will ·slip, and men would run out on a topsail yard and drop down to the earring if barefooted, when they would not do so in shoes. Most of the men liked the innovation, but we encountered objection from a few old "barnacles," who, even on the equator, would wear woolen socks, the only kind furnished by the paymaster at that time. These cases were sent to the doctor and exceptions made if he so recommended, but eventually they all became reconciled to the new style in footgear.

In 1889 I was ordered to Washington as a member of the Board of Inspection and Survey. We conducted the trials of some of the pioneer steel ships of the "New Navy," but otherwise the duties were largely of a routine and somewhat uninteresting nature. During this period the writer served at the head of a mixed commission to select a site for a naval station in northwestern United States waters, the other members being Ex-Senator Thomas C. Platt; Hon. Richard Willington Thompson of Indiana, Ex-Secretary of the Navy; Colonel Thomas Mendall, of the U. S. Army Engineer Corps, and Lieutenant A. B. Wykoff, U. S. N.

A lighthouse tender was placed at our disposal, and we inspected a number of sites near the mouth of the Columbia River and about Puget Sound. The final choice lay between Lake Washington and Bremerton. The former possessed the great advantage of fresh water, in which the underwater hulls of vessels are much more immune from deterioration and fouling than in sea water, but at that time there was no prospect of a canal being built to connect Lake Washington with Puget Sound. Many years afterwards this was done, and now vessels from sea can pass into the lake, which is an excellent place for such purposes as the laying up of the numerous destroyers at present out of commission in salt water harbors, where their bottoms deteriorate and foul rapidly.

The commission decided that Bremerton combined more advantages than any other place, and recommended the acquisition of 1,000 acres there, at a total cost of $30,000. In the subsequent Congressional debates on this item of the appropriation bill, our recommendation was severely criticised on the ground of extravagance. Senator Spooner of Wisconsin defended us against this charge. It was true that most of the existing Navy Yards were much smaller in area, yet periodically need is felt for expanding them, and the almost uninhabited nature of the country about Bremerton made the land so cheap that it seemed wiser to buy enough initially to obviate the probability of subsequent purchase at much greater cost. Moreover the 1,000 acres recommended included Kitsap Lake, fed from springs, which would assure an ample and cheap water supply for the prospective naval station.

But Congress cut the appropriation to $10,000, which permitted the purchase of only 190 acres, and could not include the lake. The folly of this pennywise economy was amply demonstrated in subsequent years when $296,000 had to be spent to enlarge the Yard by only 29 additional acres!

In 1890 I was detailed as Commandant of the Boston Navy Yard, an unusually important command for a captain. After three years there, which brought promotion to the rank of Commodore, I returned to the Board of Inspection and Survey, as its president, in 1895. During my incumbency, the *Indiana,* the first battleship built in the United States, was inspected by the board, and held her trials under its supervision.

CHAPTER XXIII

In November of 1895, I was ordered to relieve Rear-Admiral Kirkland in command of the European Squadron. Proceeding by mail steamer, with my staff, Lieutenants Hunker and Russell, we landed at Havre, and then went by rail to Marseilles, where the Flagship *San Francisco* was anchored. There an appointment as acting Rear-Admiral was received, and my flag, as such, accordingly hoisted upon taking over the command. Shortly afterwards a regular commission as Rear-Admiral was received.

My orders were to proceed direct to Alexandretta, Syria, and to remain on the coast of Asia Minor until further instructions were issued. At Smyrna, what promised to be a dreary stay was made quite pleasant by the hospitality of the many opulent English and Greek merchants, who resided in the charming suburbs of Bounabat Bouja and Cordelion, and controlled the principal trade of Asia Minor. Some of these European families had lived in this vicinity for more than a hundred years. The Turks lived in their own part of the city, and served as middle men connecting the commerce of the interior with the foreign houses at the sea port, but did little business in their own name. During this and subsequent long stops at Smyrna many pleasant acquaintances were made. I particularly remember Mr. Eliardi, a retired banker, his wife, and interesting family, who threw their house open to the Americans, and we spent frequent, enjoyable evenings in their company. One of their daughters, Domini, a charming girl of about 12 years of age, possessed great musical talent. Later she married Sir Arthur Crosfield, at one time a member of Parliament, and in the Great War she and her sister were actively interested in hospital work in London.

In April, 1896, in accordance with instructions by cable, I shifted my flag from the *San Francisco* to the *Minneapolis* at Naples, and sailed for Cronstadt, in order to represent the American Navy at the coronation of the new Tsar at Moscow. A stop at Southampton was made to receive from the mails the Navy Department's final instructions, and my diplomatic credentials as an American representative, sealed with the great seal of the State Department. Reaching Cronstadt on May 13th, the need for making calls on officials there delayed departure on the rail journey to Moscow until the 16th. My staff, comprising Fleet Captain Wadleigh and Lieutenants Hunker and Russell, accompanied me.

At Moscow we were thoughtfully met by Mr. Pierce, Secretary to the American Ambassador Mr. Breckenridge, and conducted to an excellent house which had been rented for our prospective stay of about three weeks. The whole city was gaily decorated with flags, and my Admiral's flag was soon added to the two Russian and two American flags flying from our house, which we found very comfortable. A good landau, with coachman and two fine black horses, were included in the menage, since such transportation was indispensable for complete strangers who had to attend many functions in a crowded city, but the fact that the coachman was from St. Petersburg, and knew nothing of Moscow, made it necessary to hire a chasseur, or footman, also. The latter, named Orloff, proved to be a most interesting and valuable adjunct to our party. He was gorgeously dressed; a bright overcoat with large brass buttons, a conspicuous dagger suspended from the shoulder by a great gold band, and a chapeau, which we called the "Helmet of Navarre," decorated with a big flowing blue plume. Indeed he quite outshone the Admiral and Staff, and the soldiers and policemen would touch their caps to him, but our compensation was in the facility with which he got us through difficult places; with him on the box we had easy entrée everywhere. We were also indebted to the kind assistance of Lieutenant Gourko, a son of the famous General, who was detailed to keep a watchful eye upon us, and especially to be sure that we got to our right places at the proper times.

The ceremonies attendant upon the coronation of a Tsar of Russia have always afforded a series of magnificent spectacles, and those incident to Nicholas II ascending the throne in 1896 were no exception. The immensity of the old Russian Empire, the unusual combination of religious and civic veneration in which the Tsar was held by his subjects, the contrast between high civilization and retarded development represented in the several elements of the Russian population, and the great wealth and military power of the country, all contributed to the splendor and intense interest of the event. The participants and spectators fortunately could not foresee the course of a tragic history which was to mark this occasion as the last of its kind.[1]

In accordance with the ancient custom that the Tsar and Tsarina shall reside outside of Moscow until crowned, the first of the long series of ceremonies began with the state entrance of the sovereigns into the sacred city. The writer had an excellent opportunity to view this impressive royal procession from the windows of the residence of Richard Harding Davis, then a correspondent for Harper's Weekly. First came four squadrons of

[1] The following account of my impressions in Moscow is based upon personal letters to my wife, written with no thought of their subsequent publication.

Cossacks in picturesque uniforms, with gold eagles on their helmets and black pennons on their lances, mounted on small but wiry black horses. A little distance behind, on a noble white horse, rode the Emperor alone; a dignified and kindly figure amid all the martial pomp. He was followed by the Grand Dukes and other especially distinguished men, also mounted, and dressed in varied and brilliant costumes.

Then came a series of magnificent carriages, painted in gilt á la Watteau, with footmen and pages galore. In the first, drawn by eight horses, rode the Empress Alexandra alone, looking very regal. The second, also with eight horses, contained the Dowager Empress, with the Grand Duchess Olga. They were followed by Queen Olga of Greece, and then by other members of the royal family.

The rear was brought up by the Empress' Regiment of Cossacks, with silver eagles on their helmets and red pennons on their lances, and mounted on bay horses. This regiment of household troops, together with the Emperor's Regiment, was officered exclusively by nobles, and had not been in battle since Napoleon's invasion in 1812. The procession was greeted everywhere with spontaneous enthusiasm, which together with the magnificence of the display, made the occasion one long to be remembered.

On the following day the formal coronation

took place in the Cathedral of the Assumption; located, together with the palaces and other cathedrals, inside the Kremlin, the central and formerly walled part of Moscow. Admissions were very limited, and the American party comprised only our Ambassador and Mrs. Breckenridge, Brigadier General and Mrs. McCook, and myself, in an official status, together with Mr. and Mrs. Richard Harding Davis. The two latter had had a hard fight to be admitted, in which I was very glad to be of some service.

It was necessary to start from the house as early as 7 A.M., and to join the Diplomatic Corps at the residence of the Turkish Ambassador, the dean of the corps in Moscow. There assembled about fifty carriages, many of them very handsome, with golden linings, and attended by ostentatiously liveried coachmen and footmen in wigs. The groups of carriages were arranged according to the seniority of the respective Ambassadors and Ministers, and driven in company to the Kremlin.

Alighting at the palace we walked through it to the cathedral; the way being lined with soldiers from the regiment of the Empress Dowager Marie, looking very smart in their bright cuirasses and silver helmets topped with a silver double-headed eagle. Within the cathedral, where I was indeed fortunate to have a position near the front of the spectators, all of whom had to stand during four hours, we faced a large raised platform or dais, covered with crimson velvet and bordered by a heavy gilt railing. In the center of the far side of the platform were two very handsome arm chairs over which hung a large canopy; evidently intended for the Emperor and Empress. Another chair, for the Empress Dowager, was placed a little to one side, and over this one was a smaller canopy.

It was a gorgeous assemblage. All the court gentlemen were in uniform heavily decorated with gold. On the side of the church opposite to me, were the ladies of honor in waiting upon the two Empresses; about fifty in number, dressed in Russian costume of crimson velvet. From their diamond-studded tiaras long lace veils fell down their backs. The clergy wore heavy gold vestments, and miters of gold, studded with jewels. Even the most humble of the onlookers was in a brilliant uniform or beautiful dress. This scene in the setting of the splendid old cathedral, was truly magnificent. But to appreciate the profound inspiration of the ceremonies which followed, one must also imagine the almost constant sounding of great reverberating bells from the cathedral tower, and beautiful chanting by a large choir of boys, alternating with the deep and melodious bass voice of a priest who conducted the services. For this historic occasion had a great religious as well as political significance. The Emperor of one-twelfth of the peoples of the earth combined in his person the head of their church also,

The Empress Dowager, Marie, was the first to take her place on the royal platform. She walked from the palace under a large canopy supported by eight chamberlains; her robe of silver, with an ermine collar and a long yellow silk train, lined with ermine, being carried by six gentlemen of her suite. A long curl falling down in front over her neck, a handsome collar of gems, and a beautiful little crown of diamonds, added to her regal appearance. After her arrival there was a long interim.

Finally, the Emperor and Empress Alexandra appeared in the distance. They were preceded by numerous Grand Dukes and officers, carrying the imperial standards, the imperial robes in bundles tied with yellow ribbons, the orb or globe of crystal and gold, the scepter, and the crowns; all of which were deposited on a table on the platform. The sovereigns walked under a magnificent golden canopy decorated with plumes of orange, black, and white, and carried by 32 chamberlains. The Tsar wore the uniform of a General, with his orders and a broad pink ribbon across his breast. He had a short but compactly built figure, and a good face, though firmness of character was not evident.

The Tsarina followed him closely, dressed in a comparatively simple gown of silver, trimmed with a broad pink ribbon across her breast and a single necklace. She was about an inch taller than the Tsar, and, although I did not think her handsome, was attractive in appearance, in spite of looking very tired and serious.

The arrival of the royal couple marked the beginning of an intoned religious service, during which they remained standing, crossing themselves from time to time. This was followed by a Metropolitan advancing from below the platform, placing his hands upon the Emperor's head and reading long blessings from a book; the same procedure being repeated with Alexandra. Then began the formalities of presenting the symbols of office. The Metropolitan proffered the royal robes of ermine and silk, which the Bishop, assisted by the young Duke Michael, fastened about the Tsar's neck; where the collar of St. Andrews, in diamonds, was similarly placed. Next came the crown of Russia, a mass of diamonds, about 12 inches high, with an enormous ruby supporting a diamond cross in front, which the Bishop handed to Nicholas who *crowned himself.* Then the Tsar received the scepter, and the orb of crystal and gold, as the final manifestations of supreme authority.

It still remained to crown Alexandra, who, after receiving the imperial robe, knelt in front of the Emperor. The latter handed his scepter and orb to attendants, removed the crown from his head, and with it touched the head of the Empress. Then replacing the crown upon his own head, he received another and smaller crown, a counterpart of the one worn by the Empress Dowager, and crowned Alexandra.

When the Tsar and Tsarina resumed their seats, they received the formal congratulations of a long line of distinguished personages, beginning with the Grand Duke Michael, the Tsar's brother. After this there began a protracted religious service, intoned and chanted, lasting an hour. This phase of the ceremony was terminated by one of the Metropolitans approaching the Emperor, who, laying aside his crown, scepter, and orb, proceeded down the steps, followed by the Empress, to a screen, behind which they partook of the holy sacrament. Upon their return to the throne, another religious service was conducted for a half hour, after which the final departure from the cathedral was made. The series of ceremonies had lasted three hours.

The Emperor put on his crown, took his scepter in one hand and the crystal orb in the other, and, followed by the Empress, passed out by the opposite door from which they had entered. The imperial robes were borne by Chamberlains, and the same procession of gentlemen attendants accompanied the sovereigns' departure, as upon their arrival. The Empress Dowager left next, by the same door through which she had entered, and was followed by the royal ladies-in-waiting. Then the Diplomatic Corps made their exit to the palace, where a bountiful luncheon was served to them.

Meantime the royal couple went through a more private ceremony, of venerating the ancestors of the Tsar in the Church of the Ascension and the Cathedral of St. Michaels; the latter containing the tombs of all the earlier Tsars previous to Peter the Great, who with his successors was buried in St. Petersburg. Finally, the official representatives from the different parts of the Empire were entertained by the Emperor and Empress at a state luncheon in the dining hall of the Tsars. I did not wait, with others of the foreign diplomatic group, to see the sovereigns return to their apartments after their luncheon, but being somewhat fatigued, took my carriage and went home to rest for the evening celebrations.

At 10 P.M. we started out under Orloff's guidance to see the grand illumination of the city and Kremlin. The night was perfect; mild, and no wind. Brilliant lights greeted the eye everywhere, but were concentrated principally at the Kremlin. From the bridge spanning the Naskeva River, which flows at the foot of the Kremlin wall, the sight was superb. The whole face of the crenellated wall, through a distance of about three miles, was covered with gas jets, while the towers of the five great gates were a mass of colored electric lamps, from foundation to top, where a large cross or crown surmounted all. Beyond, could be seen the numerous great cathedral and church bell towers, each a blaze of emerald and gold, or sapphire. The reflection in the river added to the splendor of a spectacle which held one spell-bound. This grand illumination was continued through three successive nights; though towards the last, dark gaps were caused by broken electric bulbs, and by the wind blowing out many of the gas jets.

On May 22nd their Majesties formally received the American Mission (including General McCook and myself), together with other foreign representatives, those of each nation being presented separately. When our turn came we were conducted first through St. George's hall, an immense and lofty room decorated in white with gilt trimmings, upon whose walls were inscribed the names of Russian regiments which had distinguished themselves in battle, and the names of officer members of the Order of St. George. Then passing through handsome metal, gilded, doors, we entered a very large gilt room, with a beautiful inlaid floor, known as "Alexander Nefsky's" room, after the ancient Russian hero. Next came "St. Andrew's" room, equally large and magnificent, in which was a throne under a great silk canopy. But the Tsar was still farther on our way, through a corridor lined with Life Guards,' and through still another large reception room, where we stopped to be presented to several princesses. The latter all spoke

English and proved very entertaining. Finally the doors to the Emperor's private apartments were swung wide open by two big black Soudanese guards, the Japanese Mission came out, and Mr. Breckenridge, General McCook and myself were ushered in.

The royal couple were standing together. The Emperor received us first, shaking hands with each in turn. After the Minister had passed on to the Empress, General McCook presented his credentials to the Tsar, and then I did the same. His Majesty spoke English perfectly and I had quite a little conversation with him, largely about America, in which subject he displayed a keen interest. While not seeming to have great decision of character, he impressed me as a man who would be a kind ruler and a good husband. The Empress Alexandra greeted me very graciously, but to my great regret, I had no opportunity to converse with her. She had a very kind and refined face, and looked very sweet, and not at all bored, though she had been standing and receiving for an hour; yet the Tsarina could scarcely be called handsome, certainly not in comparison with her sister, the Grand Duchess Serge. As soon as our audience was finished, we three retired to the door, while the remainder of the American Mission were presented, after which all withdrew together.

During the next two weeks one festivity followed another so quickly as to be quite bewildering, and I will confine my descriptions to those which were the most notable.

In the evening of the day of our presentation at Court, we attended a great spectacular opera given by the Tsar to his officers and distinguished strangers. Arriving at 7:30 P.M., according to instructions, we had an hour before the performance to examine the magnificence of the opera house. It was very large, having seats for 2,000 persons, and beautifully decorated in heavy gilt throughout. In the center of the first balcony were the spacious and highly adorned Imperial boxes. As the theatre filled with Russian officers, in bright and picturesque uniforms and decorations, ladies in superb ball dresses and handsome jewels, and foreign officers and diplomats in full uniform, it made a brilliant and animated scene. The royal party arrived at 8:30, and when the Emperor with the Empress appeared, the whole audience rose and faced their Majesties, giving the Russian cheer (a long drawn-out roar), while the great orchestra struck up the national hymn; the audience bowing repeatedly towards the royal box during the music.

This greeting finished, a superb program began with a prologue in opera called *La Vie de Tsar*. It was a wonderful combination of art and music; the chorus of about one hundred being drawn from the opera houses of both Moscow and St. Petersburg. The scene of the first act being laid in a country village, the costumes were of peasant life;

the men in ugly Russian dress looked like brigands, while on the contrary the women in bright skirts and colored head pieces were very picturesque. In the epilogue, the scene was of Moscow in the distance, and all the actors were in gorgeous court dress. At the end the whole troupe of nearly 200 struck up the national anthem, the audience rising and cheering. It was very inspiring. During the half hour intermission, a supper of ices, cakes, fruit, and champagne was served in the upper foyer. Then began a magnificent pantomime ballet, such as is rarely equaled outside of Russia. Towards its close there was supposed to be a fight between the pearls and the corals, which afforded opportunity to simultaneously display the great skill of the eighty or more performers, whose drill and dancing were perfect. The close was marked by the audience again rising and cheering repeatedly, and when at this point, the royal party left, the Emperor must have been greatly pleased in the certainty that his guests had enjoyed themselves immensely.

On the morning of May 30th, a great tragedy occurred to mar the happy spirit of the coronation celebrations. It had been arranged that at the "Fête Populaire au Rhodvuskoie," the Emperor should personally distribute a little paper bag, containing sunflower seeds, filberts, dates, candy, and a small cup, to each of his subjects who should come to receive it. The recipients were to assemble on a large plain near a specially built pavilion, from which the Emperor was to make the distribution, beginning in the early afternoon. The police seem to have under-estimated the scope of the popular response to the occasion, and perhaps also influenced by being tired out from previous strenuous duties, did not reach the pavilion until 9 A.M.

Meantime, men, women, and children from the country and city had been assembling all night, until a multitude of some 200,000 were concentrated, without any organization or supervision, each intent upon getting close enough to the pavilion to be certain of obtaining a royal gift. Probably soon after daybreak those in the rear began to press forward, and ultimately to crush those in front. The cries of the latter seem to have been interpreted in the outskirts as exultation over the receipt of presents, and to have resulted in still greater pressure from the rear. Panic soon reigned in the helpless van. Many were crushed to death, others lost their footing, especially in the several ditches, which traversed the plain, and were trampled by the mob. When the police arrived, and finally with much difficulty restored order by driving the people off the plain, the ditches were filled with dead, blood and clothing were scattered everywhere, and the air was rent with the terror-stricken cries of the maimed, and of those who had lost parents, children, brothers, and sisters. Fifteen hundred people had been killed.

Strange as it may seem, few of those who assembled later in the pavilion, by the appointed hour of 1:30, knew anything of the dreadful catastrophe. It is said that even the Emperor was not informed of it. He sat with the royal family in the top or second, story of the huge pavilion, to listen to the music rendered by a great band and some 800 chorus voices, assisted by bells and the firing of cannon. Beyond the enclosure for the musicians, a vast throng of about 300,000 had regathered to see and cheer the Tsar and to hear the music. The lower floor of the pavilion was set apart for the distinguished guests, and many notable persons were present. I had the pleasure of meeting and talking to Li Hung Chang, the Duke of Connaught, who did me the honor of asking to have me presented, the Grand Duchess of Oldenburg, Admiral Popoff, several Princesses, a number of ladies, and others whose names have escaped me.

It was only after returning to our carriages and starting home that we became aware of the tragedy. We passed two large drays loaded with corpses, and our driver who had learned the terrible news while awaiting at the pavilion, informed us of the shocking details. While listening to the music and casually chatting to each other, we had heard or seen nothing to indicate that 1,500 human beings were lying on the plain, cold in death. It is horrible to think of!

In view of this distressing tragedy it seemed

rather heartless to hold the French ball, to which 800 invitations had been issued for that evening, but probably it would have been difficult to disarrange the coronation schedule. The ball was a brilliant affair and must have been a matter of great expense. The floral decorations were gorgeous, and in one end of the immense hall was a great fountain, surrounded by palms and ferns, with the waters illuminated by various colored electric lights. Adjacent rooms were hung with pieces of superb Gobelin tapestry brought from Paris.

At first the dancing was confined to the lancers, of eight couples of royalty including the Emperor and Empress, the other guests crowding about in a great jam to look on. The Empress' gown was of her favorite cloth of silver, set off by a magnificent necklace of huge diamonds and a jeweled crown. Our Ambassador's wife remarked, "She must have a lot of crowns, because she has a different one on every time I see her!" The royal couples displayed much grace, and when their lancers were finished, waltzed up and down in a lane made for them through the crowd. Then the other couples joined in.

The room was hot, and being also fatigued I spent the time talking with various people, instead of dancing. The Princess Galitzin was very attractive and handsome, a grandmother without a grey hair in her head. The agreeable Duke and Duchess of Edinburgh were both decidedly stout.

I also had the honor of meeting the Grand Duke Alexander, a son of Vladimir, who was a first cousin of the Tsar. His mother, the Grand Duchess, whom I had met at a German dinner, gave me a pleasant smile of recognition while dancing, as did many others. A buffet was open all the evening, where light refreshments and champagne were served, and at about 1 A.M. the company sat down to supper at tables of eight. Not being hungry, and having no partner, I departed for home soon after they were seated.

On the following evening another ball took place in the Alexander Nefsky hall (already described) of the Granovistara Palace, in the Kremlin. It was a kind of polonaise, in which a royal cortège marched up and down the great hall between lines of interested spectators. At intervals the cortège stopped, and then resumed its march; the Emperor alternately choosing ladies of different Embassies for his partner, while the corresponding Ambassador marched with the Empress. The latter wore a very handsome yellow satin robe, with silver embroidery, and the great diamond necklace.

A few nights later the Tsar gave a state banquet in the great hall of St. George, the one mentioned previously as being finished in white with gilt trimmings. Only the most distinguished personages were invited, yet the Brazilian Ambassador told me he had counted 800 places at the tables.

At one end was the royal table, with all the ornaments and utensils in solid gold, while the guests of lesser rank were distributed among other tables with beautiful silver furnishings. The china was of decorated Russian gilt. Except at the royal table there were few flowers, as they were very scarce and expensive in Russia, and Russians did not seem to care much for them. At intervals through the dinner an orchestra played exquisite music from a balcony, and a tenor sang from the opera of Ernani, in a voice so magnificent that one was held spellbound as the glorious notes rang through the great hall.

I sat between Mrs. McCook and the Hon. Mrs. Monson, an English lady who was a guest of the Duchess of Edinburgh, and enjoyed the dinner very much. Upon its conclusion coffee was served in the Alexander hall and the St. Andrew's hall, and then we went out on the terrace, where a fine view of Moscow could be seen. A group of guests, principally some old Russian officers, with the wives of the Diplomatic Corps and other ladies, formed a circle, around which their Majesties passed, holding short conversations with each. The royal party left soon after, and then the dinner broke up.

On the following day, with two others, I had a charming presentation to the Empress Dowager, Marie, who was residing temporarily in the lower story of the palace, across the main entrance from the apartments of the Empress Alexandra. The great halls mentioned previously were just above. The Empress Dowager was dressed in white satin and looked very young and pretty. She lisped a little, with a foreign accent, which made her English quite attractive, and was most agreeable during our five minutes conversation, which I enjoyed very much.

During the forenoon of June 6th a great military review was held on the Champs de Mars, an immense plain outside the city and opposite the Petrovoski Palace, where the Emperor stayed before his formal entrance into the capital. When we arrived at the central pavilion, or reviewing stand, it was a truly magnificent spectacle to see 105,000 troops in full-dress uniform, massed for the ceremonies. In about an hour the Tsar and Tsarina appeared in a chariot drawn by four white horses, with riders in imperial livery, and preceded by a gorgeously attired officer, also on a white horse. They spent a good half hour in the preliminary of driving through lines of troops, and then stopped in front of the pavilion to receive the review proper.

Battalion after battalion of infantry marched by in column of companies, preserving splendid alignment, to the music of a great band stationed in front of the Emperor. After the infantry, came the artillery; twelve field pieces abreast, each drawn by six horses, matched in color by regiments. Finally the mounted troops went by in great numbers;

regular cavalry, Cossacks in their picturesque uniforms, numerous regiments of cuirassiers, with their cuirasses shining like polished silver; then the lancers and dragoons. This great review was a very impressive and brilliant affair, rightly counted as one of the principal events of all the coronation ceremonies.

In the afternoon of the same day the American Minister, General McCook, and myself had the honor of an audience with the Emperor and Empress at the palace in the Kremlin, before making our departure from Moscow. We were ushered into the great St. Andrew's hall, with which I had become so familiar as to feel quite at home! After a short wait for someone ahead of us, we passed through another room, where some cuirassier guards presented swords, and into the Red Throne room, or hall of the Order of St. Catherine, an order which only the Empress conferred. Here a few minutes' delay gave opportunity for a short chat with two Russian Princesses, whom I had met several times before, but whose names have escaped my memory.

Finally we entered the Tsar's private drawing room where Their Majesties were receiving. It seemed impossible that their heads should not have been turned by the pomp and adulation of the past weeks; yet they were as simple and pleasant in their cordiality as any ordinary persons would be to their guests. Following a few words with the Emperor,

I seized the first opportunity I had had for a talk with the Empress. She looked very tired, and left it to me to carry on a general conversation, in which I mentioned my presentation at Cowes and enquired about the health of her grandmother, Queen Victoria. On taking leave, I expressed to the Tsar a sincerely felt wish that he should have a long and prosperous reign, to which he replied by thanking me and kindly voicing a hope to see me again. The impression he left was that of a most lovable personality; as Prince Dolgorouki subsequently said to me, "I love him first because he is a gentleman, and second because he is Emperor." When our party left the palace rooms and halls, I took a last long look, realizing that I should never see them again, but little dreaming of the frightful inhumanities that were to be endured by their kindly royal occupants in the tragic maelstrom of the Bolshevik revolution.

We left Moscow with great regret. To witness the coronation ceremonies had been one of the most pleasant and interesting experiences of my life. Only a spectator could possibly appreciate the grandeur of the spectacles, or sense their inspiring associations. A contagious spirit of combined patriotism, awe, veneration, and love permeated the populace. They loved the Tsar as a man, they venerated him deeply as the head of their church, they felt awe from the fact of his unlimited power, while his personification of political and military

Russia herself, appealed strongly to their national pride and loyalty. All contributed to an atmosphere which gave to the grand pomps and forms a unique and deep significance, the influence of which dominated all who were fortunate enough to be present.

I rejoined the *Minneapolis* at Cronstadt, and towards the middle of June sailed for Helsingfors, Finland, where a stop of five days gave me a welcome opportunity of visiting my sister, Madame Etholin, at her country estate of Tavesby. Thence the ship proceeded to Stockholm. King Oscar of Sweden gave me the honor of an audience, and followed it later by a dinner at his country palace at Bernstroff, to which the American Minister and several of my officers were also invited. The Queen being ill, it was a stag affair. Before his accession to the throne King Oscar had been an officer of the Swedish Navy for many years, and consequently was thoroughly at home among naval officers. He put formality aside, and we spent a most enjoyable evening swapping yarns, in which the King, who spoke good English, did his share.

On the way out of the Baltic the *Minneapolis* stopped at Copenhagen, where, in company with the American Minister, I paid my respects to King Frederick VIII of Denmark. A few days later he invited our Minister, myself, and staff to dine at Fredemburg Palace; really a large gentlemen's villa, about 15 miles from the city. There the King presented us to Queen Louise, Princess Marie of France, and a lady-in-waiting to the Queen. This small party dined very informally, and therefore very delightfully, in the open air, under some noble beech trees, of which there were many upon the estate. I enjoyed this dinner, with its pleasant surroundings and informal conversation, together with the King of Sweden's dinner, more than any other similar party in Europe.

The Princess Marie proved especially attractive. She was very vivacious, had charming manners, and was much interested in America and Americans, since her father, the Duc de Chartres, and her uncle, the Count de Paris, had both served in our Civil War on General McClellan's staff. After dinner I said to her, "Princess, we should be much flattered if you would visit the *Minneapolis*." "I would like to very much," she replied, "but fear the King would not permit me." "May I have your permission to ask him?" "Yes indeed," she answered with evident eagerness. When we were on the point of leaving I said to the King, "It would be a special favor of your Majesty if the Princess could visit my ship." Calling Marie, he said pleasantly, "The Admiral has asked me to permit you to go on board the *Minneapolis;* if you would like to do so, you have my permission." The next afternoon, accompanied by a lady and an aide-de-camp, a Danish lieutenant, she arrived with three handsome bouquets; one for me, one for the captain, and one for the wardroom officers. After being shown about the ship, she came down to the cabin and had a jolly time with the young officers, who assisted me in entertaining her.

From Copenhagen the *Minneapolis* proceeded to the Firth of Forth, where the officers and crew had an opportunity to visit many interesting points in Scotland. Thence we sailed for the Thames River, and from the anchorage at Gravesend, London could be visited conveniently. The next stop was at Southampton, where I learned the sad news of the death of my dear mother at San Francisco, on August 21, 1896. All of her children held her in great love and veneration, and her death was a heavy loss to them.

Born in Boston, she was the daughter of Judge John Soley, who was at one time the Grand Master of the Grand Lodge of Massachusetts Freemasons. Her mother was the daughter of Colonel Samuel Henley, an officer of the Revolutionary Army, and of Catherine Russell Henley, a famous beauty, whose portrait, painted by Copley, now hangs in my library. Mrs. Henley's father was James Russell of Charlestown, the head of a family from which James Russell Lowell was descended.

My mother and her two sisters, Catherine and Mary, were very handsome, being known as the "three graces." But their beauty of character transcended beauty of person. Although of decidedly social tastes, and possessing a large circle of friends, my mother's interests centered chiefly in her family, and she was constantly with her children, both in their hours of study and of play. She was ardently patriotic and sincerely religious. Since the foundation of character necessarily comes from the home, I largely attribute whatever virtues I may possess to the inspiration of my mother's teachings and example.

At Southampton I had the pleasure of seeing my sister, Mrs. Johnson, widow of Surgeon Johnson, U. S. N., and their daughter, who had married a British officer residing at Southsea. The next stop was at Queenstown, now so well known as the main base of American overseas destroyers during the late war. I took advantage of the opportunity to visit the very picturesque west coast of Ireland, where the influence of the Gulf Stream seems to make perpetual Spring. Bantry Bay, the extreme southwest corner of Ireland, is a beautiful spot, whence the ride to Killarney can scarcely be excelled; and then there was the Lake of Killarney itself, whose praise has been justly recorded so often in poem and song.

But it was not possible to linger in interesting Ireland, for my presence was needed in the Near East, from which I had been absent nearly five months. The tendency of the Turks to persecute Armenians and Christians required the frequent influence of the Commander-in-Chief in that region. At Smyrna, it was pleasant to return to my own more comfortable quarters on board the *San Francisco,* and to renew associations with the officers of the flagship and with the very agreeable colony of Europeans ashore.

During 1897 war was brewing between the United States and Spain, and I kept in frequent communication with our Naval Attaché at London and Madrid, Commander Raymond Rodgers, as the most convenient source of intelligence for my remote station. While the Navy Department issued no instructions as to the course which the squadron should pursue in the event of hostilities naturally such a contingency received my most careful consideration. The principal Spanish force consisted of four cruisers, considerably superior in gun power, though probably somewhat slower than the four vessels under my command. On the other hand, we had an advantage in being equipped with torpedoes, while they were not. In the absence of contrary orders I did not propose to leave the Mediterranean without a fight, for which we made diligent preparations for many months, by intensive training of gun and torpedo crews and by working out the tactical details of a possible battle.

My intention was, upon declaration of war, to seek the Spanish Squadron off their base at Cartagena. With such .small forces engaged, there was little probability of our being able to gain or hold the tactically advantageous capping, or "T" position, the only condition under which a purely gunnery contest offered us reasonable prospects of success, because easily executed "head of column" changes of course by the enemy could always keep us bearing off his beam. It was therefore necessary to utilize our torpedoes if possible; and probably this could be accomplished only by forming "line abreast," and standing at full speed on a course nearly perpendicular to the enemy's column, until the range was closed to 1500 yards or less. Then a turn together through eight points would enable us to fire torpedoes, and to open with full broadside gunfire. Of course, during the approach the prospective enemy would have the advantage of broadside fire, while we would be limited to replying with only the few guns carried forward. But under the conditions of a rapid approach, and consequently of a rapid change of range, obscured by smoke, we would be difficult targets to hit, and it seemed wiser to accept the initial temporary handicap of bow fire against broadsides, for the sake of carrying our torpedoes into effective range early in the action. Otherwise, the superior Spanish gunfire might pound us to pieces at long range, before the short-range torpedoes of that period could be utilized.

In those days torpedoes were rather unreliable weapons, in fact they often manifested a disturbing boomerang tendency to curve in their supposedly straight course and select the firing vessel for their target! But this deficiency might be overcome by constant trials of the weapons and training of the personnel, and I had hopes of sinking at least one Spanish cruiser with a torpedo. If so, the gun action, which must ultimately settle the issue, would not be so one-sided, and the too common fault in naval battles of an indecisive result would be avoided. However these plans came to naught, since war did not break out until after my flag had been hauled down, and my successor had been ordered to leave the Mediterranean.

Meantime, while these preparations were in progress, the usual peace activities of the squadron were continued. Early in 1897 the *San Francisco* made a trip to Ville Franche, the former headquarters, until affairs in the East became critical, where I had the pleasure of meeting my wife who had been in Europe for some time, but too far away for me to see her. After a month, the ship sailed on the return to Smyrna, stopping en route at Naples, whence I went to Rome and had the honor of an audience with the Pope, and then with the King of Italy.

The first occasion came about in this way. The chaplain of the *San Francisco,* the Reverend Father Parks, brought to call upon me a number of young American priests, who were under instruction at the Catholic College at Rome. They were a splendid lot of young men, ardently patriotic, who, citing the instance of a private audience which the British Admiral had had with the Pope some six months previously, insisted that the American Admiral must be equally honored. Naturally I was glad to concur in this view, and the young priests, through the head of their college, Monsigneur Kennedy, laid the matter before Cardinal Rampollo. The latter refused to arrange an audience, on the ground that the Pope's health was too precarious; much to the annoyance of the young American priests, who then in some way got an "underground" message to His Holiness, the Pope. The latter notified Cardinal Rampollo that he wished to meet me and directed him to make the appointment. These preliminaries took several days, and meantime our Embassy had kindly completed arrangements for my presentation to the King, between whom and the Pope rather unfriendly relations then existed. Consequently I was in mortal dread lest the two appointed times should conflict, but luck was with me and such an embarrassing situation failed to develop.

Lieutenants Hunker and Russell accompanied me to the Vatican, where from the great gate we walked through the beautiful garden and doorway. Then passing up the grand staircase, lined with Swiss Guards in uniforms of ancient pattern, we finally reached the hall of the Cardinals. After a few minutes' wait, a door was opened by a priest who announced our names and motioned for us to enter the adjoining room. He closed the door after us and we found ourselves alone in the presence of Leo XIII, the most illustrious Pope since 1758.

His Holiness was seated in an arm chair, from which he did not rise. I approached, bowing, and introduced myself and staff. He motioned me to a seat at his right, and we carried on a conversation in French, principally about the situation in Asia Minor, in which he displayed much interest. He was dressed in a long white garment, apparently of soft flannel, and wore a heavy cross suspended from his neck by a chain. I was fascinated by the Pope's benign and serene expression, saying to myself, "Here is a saintly man if there are any such." On leaving I said to him, "Your Holiness, I am a Protestant, but would feel deeply grateful for your blessing." He graciously consented, and repeated a Roman Catholic formula with his hand on my head, while I knelt on one knee before him. We then retired and paid our respects to Rampollo, before finally leaving the Vatican. A few days after this presentation the Pope blessed a large body of sailors from the *San Francisco,* from a pulpit in Saint Peter's church.

The day following my reception by Leo XIII, I had the honor of a private audience with King Humbert at the Quirinal Palace; being presented to His Majesty by an Italian naval officer, in the absence from Rome of the American Minister. The King was a fine looking, soldierly person, and discussed public questions with me for nearly a half hour. Then he said the Queen would like to see me, and I was ushered through some state apartments to her private drawing room, where I found her with one of the ladies of the court. Queen Margarita of Savoy was the most beautiful and charming of all the crowned heads that it was my good fortune to meet in Europe. We had an enjoyable chat on general subjects. It so happened that her brother, an officer of the Italian Navy, had recently visited the United States, where most of his time had been spent in Philadelphia, and his letters home had given glowing accounts of his reception in that city. Consequently the Queen was curious to know all about Philadelphia. The audience with this attractive lady was much too short for a susceptible sailor.

As the Missionary Board at home were constantly urging the Navy Department to keep our naval forces united on the Asia Minor coast, I did not like to linger too long in pleasant Italy, and the *San Francisco* soon returned to her old post at Smyrna. In the spring we made a flying visit to Athens to witness the first of the modern Olympic Games. A general invitation had been sent abroad to participate in these games, to be held in the new stadium, reconstructed, through the generosity of a wealthy Greek merchant, of the same size and on the same site as the original. Not many foreign athletes responded, and America was represented by only about twenty students from Princeton University.

The principal event was the Marathon race, which occupied most of the first day. There were many competitors, but it was won by a Greek shepherd, who finished some distance ahead of the others. It was an inspiring scene as he came running into the great stadium. The whole vast multitude of spectators seemed to go crazy with delight, gesticulating wildly, and roaring and shouting at the top of their voices. The victor was led up to King George, who crowned him amid great cheers. That a Greek had won the principal prize, so excited the patriotic ardor of the ladies of the Greek nobility, that it is said the young shepherd received offers of marriage from many of them! The second day of the games was taken up with numerous trials of strength and skill in walking, running, jumping, throwing the discus, etc., in which the Princeton athletes were conspicuously successful; so much so that some officers from the *San Francisco* gave them a "roaring blowout" at Pireus, to celebrate the American victory.

In the early summer we made another comparatively short trip from Smyrna to the north of Europe. A part of this cruise was spent at Havre, and I availed myself of the opportunity to visit my family in Paris. They were scheduled to return to the United States in September, so before leaving them again I took them across the Channel in the

San Francisco to Southampton. Returning south the *San Francisco* made pleasant stops at Lisbon and Algiers; but my pet lambs, the Armenians, could not be neglected too long, and the remainder of the year had to be passed in the vicinity of Smyrna. The year 1898 had scarcely begun before we sailed for Ville Franche, where Rear-Admiral John C. Howell was to relieve me from the command in European waters.

On the way we went up the Adriatic to Venice, which had not been recently visited by any ships of the squadron. The yacht of the ex-Empress Eugenie being in port, I sent the Flag-Lieutenant on board with my compliments, and the next day she returned the courtesy by visiting the *San Francisco,* accompanied by two of her lady companions. They spent some time at tea in the cabin; during which all of the officers came in to pay their respects. The Empress was very gracious, and in spite of an undercurrent of sadness and depression, the famous charm of her personality gave us a very delightful afternoon.

Reaching Ville Franche in due time, on February 6th, the statutory date of my retirement from active service on account of age, I hauled down my flag and turned over the command of the European Squadron to Admiral Howell; thus ending a career of forty-seven years on the active list of the Navy of my country.

CHAPTER XXIV

CONCLUSION

Since these memoirs have been prepared primarily to record the more important incidents of my active service in the Navy, I shall not dwell upon the twenty-five years which have elapsed since retirement, and which have brought no special events except those of a purely personal or family nature.

In 1905 I met with a great bereavement in the death of my dear wife, Ellen Shepley Selfridge; the devoted mother of my four sons, George, Russell, Harold, and Duncan. In 1907 I married my present wife, who was Miss Gertrude Wildes of Boston, and she has blessed my declining years with inspiring devotion. It was principally due to her interest in my naval career, and to her repeated urging, that I undertook to write these memoirs, which she believed would be valued as highly by my children as by herself.

Throughout all these years of retirement, though denied participation in the Navy's notable activities, my interest in that splendid organization has continued unabated. None but a naval officer could fully understand the devotion of another officer to their common service. The close unity of thought and action that binds our profession into a great fraternity has no parallel among civilians, since in naval life there is absent that keen competition between individual practitioners, which is so common to the civil professions and to the industrial world generally.

The Navy has ever before it the compelling need of joint action in an inspiring cause; the honor and security of the Country must be always in its thoughts. Like the Army, the Navy's unifying cause is rooted in the great sentiment of patriotism —loyalty to Country; but in the Navy, due to greater activity abroad, this influence is more powerfully at work during long intervals of peace. Moreover, the dangers and hardships of life at sea have a strong tendency to create a peculiar bond of mutual sympathy among all those who follow it. Thus service unity, bred in loyalty to the Country, is the very essence of the Navy.

It is this complex which creates among naval officers a devotion to their organization which has its counterpart only in religious and family devotion. This is the origin of that wonderful Navy spirit, handed down by Paul Jones and other early founders, and conspicuously nurtured in 1812 and in the Civil War; a spirit which instinctively manifests itself in every official act of a naval officer, and, regardless of individual capacity or merit, promotes success in all important undertakings of the United States Navy.

Upon bringing this account of my life to a close, I cannot permit the occasion to pass without adding how much I am indebted to my friend Captain Dudley W. Knox, United States Navy, for his assistance in unraveling the skeins of my memory, and with his well-known literary ability, weaving those skeins into these memoirs.